Divorce:
Prevention or Survival

JAMES F. BROWN, JR.

Divorce: Prevention or Survival

by
William V. Arnold
Dixie McKie Baird
Joan Trigg Langan
Elizabeth Blakemore Vaughan

The Westminster Press
Philadelphia

Copyright © 1977 The Westminster Press

All rights reserved—no part of this book may be reproduced in any form without permission in writing from the publisher, except by a reviewer who wishes to quote brief passages in connection with a review in magazine or newspaper.

Scripture quotations from the Revised Standard Version of the Bible are copyrighted 1946, 1952, © 1971, 1973 by the Division of Christian Education of the National Council of the Churches of Christ in the U.S.A., and are used by permission.

First edition

Published by The Westminster Press ®

Philadelphia, Pennsylvania

PRINTED IN THE UNITED STATES OF AMERICA

9 8 7 6 5 4 3 2 1

Library of Congress Cataloging in Publication Data

Main entry under title:

Divorce: prevention or survival.

    1. Divorce—United States. 2. Marriage—United States. 3. Marriage counseling—United States. 4. Interpersonal relations. I. Arnold, William V., 1941–
HQ834.D58   301.42'84   77–22066
ISBN 0–664–24142–5

To Our Parents

Contents

PREFACE   9

INTRODUCTION   11

Part One. BEFORE DIVORCE

1. Early Warning Signals   17
   Selecting a Counselor   28
2. Serious Warning Signals   31
3. Money and Marriage   42
4. Sex and Marriage   49
5. Divorce and the Church   54
6. Decision-Making   58
7. Limbo   72

Part Two. AFTER DIVORCE

8. Now That I'm Separated, How Will I Make It?   83
   Loneliness   85
9. A New Home and a Different Income   89
   Where Will I Live?   89
   How Can I Meet Expenses?   94
10. New Relationships   97
    Dealing with Your Children   97
    Dealing with Your Ex-Spouse   109
    Dealing with Friends, Social Life, and Relatives   113
11. Dating   116

Preface

We are divorced and have been for several years. After much struggling and confusion, we now find life rewarding. The trauma of divorce is a thing of the past.

Our development after our divorces is due largely to our having been able to share the problems and feelings that resulted from the destruction of our marriages and the restructuring of our lives.

The sharing was done in a "divorce group" which was originated and guided by Dr. William V. Arnold, who was at that time Minister of Pastoral Care and Counseling at Second Presbyterian Church, Louisville, Kentucky. Bill was aware that many of his parishioners were becoming divorced. He therefore formed the group for divorced persons to help them understand their divorces and re-create their lives in a healthy and constructive manner.

We three were the charter members. We attended weekly meetings for two years, and as the "group" progressed we were amazed at several findings—the circumstances surrounding the divorces of all of us were different but the breakdowns of marriages fit a similar pattern. We also shared many of the same feelings while married. During our "rebirth," each of us went through the same stages, having similar feelings. Because of these shared experiences we all derived comfort that each of us wasn't "weird" after all. We know that many of you have the same concerns, worries, and feelings.

The three of us, along with Bill, wrote this book for those of you who are getting a divorce and also for those of you who might gain insight and be able to turn your marriage around. If your marriage cannot be held together, perhaps our efforts will help you to work through divorce to your best advantage. We consider ourselves "successful divorcées" and therefore want to share our discoveries so that you might have the advantage of our experience during your restructuring period. We want you to feel that you have companions and to know that you are not alone or "weird." We know; we have been there; we are still there; we are divorced.

Dixie McKie Baird
Joan Trigg Langan
Elizabeth Blakemore Vaughan

Introduction

In any bookstore these days you will find a section devoted to marital conflict or divorce. The subject is obviously a best-seller, and many writers are taking full advantage of it. In the midst of so many books about marital conflict, divorce, and family relationships, the question naturally occurs, Why another one?

Our answer is twofold. First, when the authors of this book were participating in a divorce group, there wasn't any publication really descriptive enough—without an ax to grind—to be helpful in dealing with day-to-day issues of survival in the aftermath of divorce. Second, there was a need for a book to be written by those who had experienced divorce rather than by those who had only observed it. The chapters are not simply words *about* divorce; they are words *by* the divorced. More important than the analytical structure is the firsthand identification of the experiences *and* the insights that have come out of dealing with them.

This introduction will explore some frames of reference that have been valuable in working through these experiences. Some will be easily recognized. Others are departures from the issues that are commonly discussed.

It Doesn't Just Happen. Divorces develop. That's no news to most persons. However, many do not see divorce coming. Numerous writers have attempted to describe stages that precede divorce, pointing out that divorce is more than a matter of "not being right for each other" or the marriage not being "made in heaven."

The perspective that has been most helpful to us is that of developmental psychology. We have traced the pilgrimage of relationships that dissolved, with the hope that our findings will lead to some preventive maintenance for others. Our purpose is more than to console those who have divorced, though that is important. It is also to provide some signals that may head off continued development of trouble in a marriage.

Developmental psychology holds that as individuals and relationships move through phases or stages, each new stage calls for consideration, planning, and decision-making. Individuals can make their plans privately. Relationships cannot! Two people cannot, if they are married, make private plans and expect the other to "know." If George decides that the pressure to wash the dishes is more than he can bear but never says so out loud, then Martha will soon fall into the trap of sweetly asking him to do the dishes and then being amazed, angry, or crushed at his unfeeling, categorical rejection. A battle may ensue that could well have been headed off by a simple discussion about the various responsibilities around the house and who was most willing to handle them.

If George and Martha never work that one out, there will be later incidents. When they move from the stage of the two-person family to the arrival of a child, the child when older may well be the next victim of the parents' failure to handle the simple matter of the delegation of responsibilities, either through being loaded with all the undesirable ones or listening to a constant hassle, with mother and father teaching, in effect, that home responsibilities are a major arena for battle. The child will soon learn to enter in.

Anytime a phase or stage is not dealt with successfully, all phases thereafter will be affected, really contaminated. For example, if at the beginning of a marriage one partner is insistent and the other, in order to avoid conflict, is compliant, though unenthusiastic, then later stages of the marriage that call for joint planning and mutual decision-making are in for trouble. Why? Because the marriage was not begun that way. A model, or norm, has already been set that works against mutuality and cooperation. Whenever one partner is displeased with a later decision, the feeling (expressed or unexpressed) may be, "You always make the decisions," or, "You've always been too weak to make one."

The message of a developmental perspective is, "Do your homework." It takes work to maintain a relationship. It takes work at every stage: the decision to marry; the decision on where to live; the question of children, whether, how many, and when. People must "go to the trouble" of discussing, planning, sharing, etc., if they want to *insure* (not guarantee) a productive, fulfilling experience together. It is true that things will "run along" without checking, but it raises the odds that they might "run aground." Never assume that a marriage is guaranteed to be successful. Always check the foundations at the various stages.

Ages and Stages. Our experience has been that there do seem to be identifiable stages of development, or, better, deterioration when a marriage proceeds toward divorce. The major stages we have identified are: "early warning signals" and "serious warning signals." If these signals are not recognized and dealt with, persons may find that they are unable to extract themselves from a bad situation. If the signals are recognized and dealt with, a person has the option of attempting to reverse the process or move on into "decision-making." While in "decision-making" there is still time to save a marriage. If the decision does come to divorce, each individual moves into an interim stage called "limbo" and from there into "Now that I'm alone, how will I make it?"

In the following chapters we describe these warning signals, because they are just that. Once begun, the die is *not* cast. The process can be reversed. We can learn from the warning signals and make commitments to change. The real lesson that comes from developmentalism is that solutions can develop just as deterioration can.

Communication. That is another popular word these days. What does it mean? Our experience has been that it really revolves around the issue of trust. Where there is mistrust, there will be deterioration. Mistrust often reveals a fear of being hurt in the process of sharing feelings. At the same time, there is a constant concern about "What are you not telling me?" Mistrust seeks quick solutions because it is uncomfortable with time. That kind of thinking is fed in our culture by romanticism and technology which teach us that we can get anything we want and get it fast. So, when we find out that there are differences with our mate, and they don't get solved quickly, we then feel they are not solvable. We tend to view problems and differences as final instead of as warning signals. Thus, we don't work on them.

If a wife wants to be cuddled at night, and a husband views that as an invitation to intercourse, a couple have several options. One is to try to get both needs met. Another is to view it as "an irreconcilable difference" and never work on it. A third is to trust that each will eventually take the other's needs seriously. A fourth option is to "put up with it" because there are other parts of the relationship that make it worthwhile to live with the differences or discomfort.

This is what communication or trust is basically about—a willingness to come to an understanding on something, even if it isn't "solved"; a willingness to share feelings though it may be painful; a willingness to wait because we can count on a partner to deal with issues. All the issues that have to be faced in a marriage focus on the ability of two individuals to understand and to be understood.

How Do I Love You? How do we talk about understanding each other in practical terms? You cannot define love. You cannot prescribe a list of duties. You have to have a willingness to trust and discuss.

For instance, is it *mostly* all right with you if your children acquire many of the personality characteristics of your spouse? If you are struck down by some illness or accident that incapacitates you, are you willing for your spouse to make all the decisions about your welfare? Can you find such thoughts acceptable, even if you have differences? If you don't feel those things, you don't have cause for divorce, you have a warning that some work needs to be done.

When and if the work is done and there is still much misery, then it is time to think more seriously about what is happening and to talk about divorce. That is what Chapters 1 and 2 are about: how to recognize those warning signals *early,* instead of late. And if you find them, what do you do?

WILLIAM V. ARNOLD

Part One

BEFORE DIVORCE

CHAPTER 1

Early Warning Signals

What happens in marriages that break down? Have you ever been aware of trying to fool yourself? We fool ourselves lots of times, and not always intentionally. When we hear bad news, such as an accident or a death, our reply is, "You don't mean it!" Or, "What did you say?" Then, if the event really bothers us, there is still a time when we avoid talking about it. We stay busy with distracting activities to avoid recognizing or dealing with what has happened.

If you've done that, you know already what we mean by early warning signals. They are the initial clues in a marriage that something is happening or has happened that we don't like. They are things of which we are aware but not aware.

Jane and Bill were just beginning another day. After a quick breakfast, Bill headed out the door saying, "I'll call you if I can make it home for supper, but don't plan on it." For the umpteenth time, Jane started to ask the reason for the late hour, but, not wanting to repeat an old argument, she sighed and planned another lonely evening at home. She started to think about it again as he drove off but then shrugged and resolved that they would have to work on the problem—sometime!

That little vignette includes some of the major early warning signals that constitute the breakdown of communication in a marriage. They are little at first inspection, but the danger is that they will grow. The further danger is that their smallness seems so apparently harmless that we, even when worried, confine ourselves to an internal lecture not "to be so picky" about our mate and what we expect the relationship to be like. In essence, we don't act. We just speculate, mind-read, and worry. We do not communicate.

In all healthy relationships there will be early warning signals. It is important for you to see the signals and decide on ways to deal with them rather than falling into the syndromes we will mention. If you already have early warning signals that you feel can't be corrected, it's important to understand what went wrong. We have found that early warning signals can appear at various times and for a variety of reasons in different relationships. Some signals may occur before marriage, others within early marriage or in a healthy relationship of long duration. The reasons they may appear also vary with each set of circumstances. However, when they appear is not as important as recognizing a signal and deciding to do something. Many persons spend years brooding on how, where, or when, instead of taking positive action. They literally "choose" to avoid solving a problem by sticking with their unsuccessful methods. The kinds of action you can take will be discussed later.

We have broken down the early warning signals into four categories:

1. *Denial*—Lack of honesty and integrity with one's self
2. *Avoidance*—Not talking over with your partner concerns about the relationship
3. *Repetition*—Attempting to discuss problems but achieving no lasting solution
4. *Detachment*—Lack of true commitment to the quality of the relationship

We recognize that these are not strict or distinct categories. They overlap, and the following examples will tend to fall into more than one category. Think of them as ways of getting a handle on the feelings involved. Recognize them as choices being made, more often passively than actively.

FIDDLEDEEDEE, I'LL THINK ABOUT THAT TOMORROW—Denial

The choice here is "I will be busy, and I will choose *not* to do something about or identify the underlying feelings that are troubling me." Jane shrugs and puts off her problem-solving. Many of us prefer to ignore things that are troublesome. The attitude prevails that "If I don't see it, it might go away," or, "It really isn't important," or, "I'll deal with that later." This constitutes a lack of self-honesty over what are usually very real apprehensions.

The apprehensions relate to many different sets of circumstances. Some examples are concern over the basis for the relationship, a major change within a family, or complacency.

One partner may be vaguely worried about why he chose the other. There may have been social pressure, either real or self-imposed. The engagement may have been announced or everybody knew a marriage was imminent; therefore they succumbed to the fear of ending the relationship and creating an embarrassment.

Pressure may have come from otherwise reliable sources such as, "He is such a wonderful man, how could you not snap him up?" Some persons may marry to prevent hurting the other or con themselves into thinking, "He loves me; therefore surely I love him, too." Some persons choose marriage as an escape from loneliness, an unhappy home situation, boredom, a present bad marriage, or they directly rebel against members of their family or the Establishment. The feeling that "Anything is better than what I have now" may develop, preventing an accurate look at the quality of the relationship.

In working marriages, when a major change happens, some couples have not maintained the network for productive communication and are not able to cope with the trauma. The trauma can be job changes, changes in life-style, a death in the family, or children leaving home. The issues and their effects can be submerged and essentially ignored.

In other working marriages of long duration there need not even be a trauma. The partners may become complacent about each other and what they have been successful in building. Through lack of attention, troubling incidents may occur that are ignored, starting the breakdown. An example could be that as life changes, each partner may adjust to changes by establishing new interests independent of the other. While this can be healthy, it can also become destructive if the interests become totally absorbing, leaving no time or room for the other.

In any of these situations, it becomes far simpler "not to think" than to face some undesirable facts and work toward a solution. To postpone thinking is an early signal, but you can't postpone forever!

MUM'S THE WORD—*Avoidance*

"I choose to analyze the situation, and I choose *not* to discuss it with my partner."

Susan and George have no children. They both work to provide an adequate income that gives them an opportunity for outside interests and hobbies. George has become absorbed in sailing. Susan is interested in tennis. They do not share these interests. Susan often worries: "We work apart all week and now play apart on weekends. Is this good? We seem to be sharing less and less." As time goes on, she broods as each weekend approaches. She wonders if George enjoys her company or has chosen sailing to avoid her. She considers asking him and discussing the issue. Perhaps they could develop a mutual interest. Finally, she chooses not to mention her concern. "Do I really want to know if George doesn't care to be with me?" Or, "I'm concerned, but is this really all that important?"

This signal is different from the first in that you are aware of the existence of a problem, accept the fact that it is a problem, but then will not discuss it. The concern can relate to almost any subject, such as money, life-style, children, lack of attention and support, or occasional behavior of the other. Some of the reasons, we have discovered, that we choose to remain silent are fear of "rocking the boat," of being crowned "the problem child" by the other, a lack of confidence in one's own judgment, or a lack of trust in the other to respond positively. Other persons are reluctant to speak up because they feel unable to express their concerns or feelings. Also, some, not recognizing it as an opportunity for growth, avoid the possibility of conflict at any cost.

Within a marriage that has been successful for a short time or for many years, circumstances may develop that concern one or both partners. They may tuck them away, hoping the ship will right itself when the wind stops blowing. An example could be the birth of children. This will always change a couple's life, and major adjustments need to be made. The couple need to create time to be together alone, whereas before it was there for the taking. One couple handled this well by occasionally hiring a sitter, then driving to the parking lot of a local shopping center to sit and talk for hours.

A child may develop the habit of climbing into bed with the parents during the night, preventing a closeness that was enjoyed before. This may be ignored on the surface but be upsetting to both underneath. Instead of working out a solution, the parents might choose, by not discussing it, to leave the situation as it is. Each may hope the other partner will solve the annoyance, or assume that it will end eventually.

The need for sharing additional responsibilities both physically and emotionally can demand a change. A couple might buy their first house or a larger house, creating the need for a reevaluation and redistribution of the work load. There is a new yard to cut and hedges to trim, larger floors to wax, and more windows to wash. If there is no discussion and mutual agreement of who will assume which responsibility, the partner who meets the physical demands "because it needs to be done" may find resentment beginning to build toward the other. Often in a marriage in which one partner assumes most of the work load, the pattern also applies to more than the house, such as caring for the children, handling the money, and making the major decisions.

Another example is when children leave home, lessening the work load for the wife and creating a void in the lives of the partners. If they are not able to discuss and create new areas of challenges, together and separately, they have missed an opportunity for a new or renewed closeness and instead have allowed the crumbling process to begin.

HERE WE GO AGAIN—Repetition

"I choose to discuss and perhaps fight, but I also choose *not* to solve the problem."

Ed and Julie constantly battle over his lack of help around the house and yard. Julie often tells Ed: "I do everything. I clean; I cook; I wash; I iron; I sew; I cut the grass; I trim the bushes; I take care of the children. What do you do? You sit; you read; you watch TV; you eat what I cook; and then you play golf all day Saturday. Please help me out." Ed's response is: "I also work forty hours a week so you can have a house to clean, yard to cut, clothes to iron, and food to cook. I'm tired when I get home. I need a change of pace on Saturday. But O.K., I see your point. I'll help out more." Julie and Ed have voiced their anger and frustration. Ed has said he'll help, but you may notice there has been no real communication. Julie has not stated her feelings, nor has Ed. While Ed says he will help, they have not worked out an agreement on who will do what in the future. They both know that nothing more has been accomplished other than an argument. Sure enough, three weeks later Julie says, "Ed, when *are* you going to cut the grass?" Here we go again!

Many of us will find that we are called upon to deal with recurring problems throughout our relationship. This is not unusual or in any way threatening if we succeed in dealing with the situation with mutual satisfaction and agreement. A problem child might be an example, creating many situations that the parents handle together over a period of years. Financial trouble can constitute another type of recurring problem that needs to be resolved, even if only temporarily. This need not cause a hazard to a healthy relationship, but can wreak havoc in a partnership that is not successful in resolving each adjustment as it happens. (See Chapter 3, "Money and Marriage.")

A young husband may insist that his wife not work, because he feels that he is the "breadwinner" of the family and that "a woman's place is in the home." His ego may prevent him from understanding that his wife may want to work in order to bring in some extra income or to seek more fulfillment in her life. Their discussions always end in his stubborn refusal to let her work. Over the years serious resentment builds as she pushes her interest into the background.

Like Julie and Ed, some couples will try discussing problems and find that nothing between them is resolved. At first it might seem that they have reached an understanding, but in time the same behavior or attitude of one or both resurfaces, indicating that the problem has not been worked through at all. The focal point is *how* a problem is dealt with, not how often it recurs or how serious it is. A behavior pattern may be established of continually rehashing the same old thing, with promises of "You are right," or "I'll do better," or "Damn it, I tried, but you didn't." The original problem becomes the secondary issue. The major issue is the unsuccessful mechanics that are used and reused in dealing with an issue. This can become a habit of a lifetime, creating feelings of frustration, anger, uselessness, or disinterest. Some of us may continue this for the duration of the relationship; others may choose the "Mum's the Word" approach, since they feel that it won't do any good to talk and that "things and people don't change." This can be a preconceived attitude or can develop as a result of patterns already established in the relationship. In any case, the beginning of loneliness will creep in.

Of major importance is *how* a problem is dealt with. The method of dealing with a problem is more important than the problem itself. Some problems won't go away, so we must find a positive way of handling them so they are not allowed to affect the relationship negatively.

Some wives feel they do not receive the attention or support they need. Their husbands may be independent and have a variety of outside interests that the wives are either unable or unwilling to share. This issue may be discussed many times and attempts may be made by the husband to "give up golf" on Sundays or not "work late every night," but eventually he will slip back into his old routine. On the other hand, the husband may have suggested an alternate solution by encouraging his wife to join him in some of his activities. She may immediately reject the offer or "try" but find she "really doesn't enjoy" what he does. This can become an issue that is raised almost on a regular basis or be verbally dropped, creating intense feelings.

In summing up the "Here We Go Again" category, we would say it seems that if this behavior pattern is established, it is indicated that one or both of the partners are unable or unwilling to make adjustments to situations or concessions to the needs or wishes of the other. This demonstrates an unwillingness to be sensitive to the other. No doubt there are situations that will recur, but *how* they are faced is the difference between "Here we go again" and constructive resolution.

I DON'T REALLY CARE—Detachment

"I choose not to care about it," or "I choose not to let my partner know I care."

Martha and Jim are newly married. Jim is an easygoing, open person who likes to share his thoughts and feelings. He often comes home wanting to sit and tell Martha about his day, his triumphs or disappointments. Martha, on the other hand, is more interested in having dinner promptly at six o'clock so she can "get it over with." For several months Jim perseveres. He tells Martha often: "Honey, why don't you chat with me before dinner and tell me about your day, too? It makes me feel rushed to shovel down dinner as soon as I get home. I feel unimportant when you don't want to talk or share." He may even offer a compromise: "Let's have a late dinner just two nights a week." Martha is unrelenting. "Jim, you know I hate to cook and want it over with, and why should we talk about trivia?" Jim eventually gives up. He tells himself: "I don't really care. Martha has her rights, too."

This warning signal or attitude can come from two sources. One is the fear of trust or commitment, a fear brought with us from past experiences. We have built a wall and are unwilling or unable to open up to become vulnerable to possible hurts or disappointments. The other source can relate directly to the relationship, how it is structured and how successful we have been in dealing with problems. If we have not succeeded in resolving or handling issues, we may take the approach that we didn't really care anyway.

If a concerned partner tries to deal with the other on any issue and the continual response, verbally or through actions, is "I don't really care," feelings of uselessness, frustration, and being unloved or not cared for will develop.

If one partner is ill and in need of attention and care and the other continues to conduct life in the usual manner, not offering sympathy or help, the ill person can lie in a bed of misery—the misery being directed at the helplessness of their situation, not at the illness itself. A young mother comes down with the flu and cannot tend to the children or daily chores. The father is resentful of her situation and chooses to let the family struggle on while he continues to conduct his life to his own liking.

A husband likes to have time alone with his wife when he comes home from work before they have dinner with the children, but she refuses to comply, being disorganized and "not ready" when he arrives.

If events like these and others continue to occur, the self-defense of one of the partners might easily become "I don't really care." Rather than become comfortable with a situation that really doesn't help or meet the need, the partner will unhappily start withdrawing and stop counting on the other.

ACTION

"I choose to change circumstances, methods of communication, or myself."

Any of the early warning signals may come at any time and for many different reasons. When and why is irrelevant at first. What is important is that in marriages headed toward divorce or chronic unhappiness some or all of these warning signals begin to appear, becoming dominant as time goes on.

When a signal appears, it is important to see it and decide on ways to deal with it, rather than fall into the syndromes we have mentioned.

Issues that are discussed and worked through may not always have results to the liking of both partners. If you are able to accept the "shortcoming" of the other and become tolerant and comfortable or are able to concede to the wishes of the other, harboring no bad feeling, the marriage remains healthy. Preserving integrity may mean coming to accept differences and adjusting to them.

One partner may find travel an important ingredient for his life. The other much prefers to stay home but is willing to give in graciously and take off for other lands.

One partner may be extremely neat and organized, the other messy beyond redemption. The neat partner, while acknowledging the good qualities of the other, may be able to adjust and live in the "horror" of a messy house or continually clean up after the other, harboring no resentment.

Acceptance should not be confused with resignation. If you become resigned to something, it is usually with some unwillingness. Feelings of resentment may result.

A method that can be implemented to bring about a major and usually a positive change is the use of "That's your problem." Its aim is to avoid the pattern of one partner becoming "the decision maker." The method simply is to establish ownership of a problem and expect the responsible partner to handle it. If the problem is overdrinking, overspending, etc., and the partner not directly involved refuses to "take over," the unhappy partner will have to cope. This may seem harsh and unfeeling, but in reality it can become an extremely supportive act. It is not provoked out of lack of interest but more by the desire to jog the other partner into new action. Such a procedure is delicate. "That's your problem" can easily be interpreted as "I don't care." When there is difficulty in the relationship already, the response of the other partner may well be an accusation of detachment and lack of interest. That is why support is so important. There are times of crisis in which one does need another person to provide guidance, structure, and advice. But those times are the exception rather than the norm. For real action in the direction of health, a kind of collaboration needs to happen instead of a leaning operation by one partner on the other. Action that brings health will come out of discussion, sometimes peaceful and sometimes agonizing, in which both persons contribute a part of the decision. Action that comes out of one partner's regularly telling the other what to do is a result of dependency that offers more promise for failure. "That's your problem" is a means of demanding that the one partner contribute a share in the decision. But it should be accompanied by "And I'll support you in *your* deciding how to deal with it."

FEELINGS

Feelings as well as communication and actions constitute the basis for the relationship, present and future.

You may have noticed that feelings that develop as a result of the lack of communication of acceptance are at first temporary. They surface only when a particular problem arises, but as time goes on and nothing important is resolved, the feelings become more profound and continuing.

Because of either the lack of communication or the lack of results from attempted communication, a feeling of loneliness begins to develop within you, your partner, or both.

You might feel isolated from the other, either through self-imposed actions or because you are forced into it through lack of support or cooperation from the other. Your loneliness develops into a more intense state and results in depression, anger, martyrdom, confusion, apathy, boredom, or withdrawal. "Why can't I get through?" or "Why do I always stir up trouble?" "Why can't I be happy and accept things the way they are?" Martyrdom can be directed at the family—"Why do I always have to do everything around here and never receive help, appreciation, or support?" Confusion implies "Help!" "What is wrong?" "Why won't things improve?" "What is wrong with me?" "I am miserable, somebody do something!"

When the feelings become this intense and consistent and a major change doesn't occur, either through a concerted effort by both partners or outside help, the relationship has moved into the serious warning stages.

HOMEWORK

1. Set aside a block of time (about thirty minutes) when you *probably* won't be interrupted.
2. Recall your most recent disagreements or concerns with your partner.
3. Evaluate whether you handled those incidents as one of the "early warning signals."
4. Tell your partner, when both of you have time to finish, about your findings.
5. *Decide together* what you will do about any undesirable outcomes in the future. You may decide to seek the help of a counselor.

SELECTING A COUNSELOR

It is advisable that anyone who is considering a divorce or is unhappy in marriage see a counselor before taking another step. Divorce is a life decision that involves others than yourself.

Many divorcing persons continue to get counsel throughout the divorce and for a period thereafter. Counseling can help in many ways: understanding what went wrong in the marriage, how divorce affects children, how emotions can cloud issues. It also helps greatly in the restructuring of life and in deciding whether to remarry.

How to Select a Counselor. Deciding to see a counselor is a momentous decision. Most of those in the profession would agree and say that the earlier in the process of dealing with your situation you decide to see a counselor, the better your chances are for a successful solution. Agonizing can become so strong a habit that it becomes more and more demanding of your energy. Consequently, less and less of your energy is available to concentrate on what's *causing* the agony. See a counselor early. This is not a sign of weakness; it is a sign of intelligence.

Once you decide to seek professional help, two steps need to be taken. The first is to find a qualified counselor; second, find a qualified counselor *you like!*

Taking care of step one is primarily a matter of checking credentials. Credentials can vary a great deal. One of the problems is that in many states there are no requirements for performing marriage and family counseling. One only has to hang out one's shingle. There are many professional organizations that have specific requirements for membership. (Addresses for the three mentioned here are given at the end of this chapter.) Among ministers, for instance, the Association for Clinical Pastoral Education and the American Association of Pastoral Counselors are reputable organizations by which one may be certified. Be sure that the person is *certified,* not simply a member. The higher levels of certification are acting supervisor, full supervisor, fellow, or diplomate. Another organization is the American Association of Marriage and Family Counselors. It is multi-disciplinary and includes ministers, social workers, and attorneys. Medical specialists include family practice and gynecology, as well as psychiatry. Of course, in most states psychologists and psychiatrists must meet certain licensure requirements to practice, and you should make sure that they have done so. Membership in the AAMFC is indicative of a special interest the person has in the arena of marriage and family problems.

Finding a qualified counselor you like is a matter that may take a little longer. Most important, you should feel a sense of trust in the counselor. That may take a little time to develop. It doesn't simply mean that you agree with him or her. After all, if you are just looking for someone who agrees with you, you can find that somewhere else and probably at a cheaper price. You should feel that this person cares about you, is willing to push you at some points and be supportive at others, recognizes the importance of *your* making some decisions, and makes you analyze potential decisions to see the dangers and the advantages of them. There are some counselors who are simply interested in your making a decision, irrespective of results. Avoid them!

In short, find a counselor with whom you seem to mesh and feel a willingness to work. That is very much a matter of finding two personalities that can work together, for there will be very qualified counselors with whom that doesn't happen. Give the process some time, but if things don't seem to click, talk about it. Research has shown that more depends on the relationship between counselor and client than on the particular technique used by the professional.

Professional Associations. The names and addresses of the three professional associations mentioned in the preceding section are as follows:

Association for Clinical Pastoral Education, Interchurch Center, Suite 450, 475 Riverside Drive, New York, N.Y. 10027

American Association of Pastoral Counselors, 3 West 29th Street, New York, N.Y. 10001

American Association of Marriage and Family Counselors, 225 Yale Avenue, Claremont, Calif. 91711

CHAPTER 2

Serious Warning Signals

How do you know when things have moved from the early stage to the serious stage? Ann and John sat down in a counselor's office. They described a history of two years of dating, three years of marriage. John had noticed that Ann didn't talk as much and their interest in sex had dropped to weekends. He had tried to bring up the subject with her, but his work load had increased and she was three months pregnant. Usually the conversation would repeat itself; they would both agree to "do more things together" but would then lapse back into the same routine. One night he frightened himself when he jumped up with fist doubled and screamed, "I'm sick of your bitching!" and stormed out. The next night he came home late and drunk. She began to brood over whether she had driven him to this. Both had the problem on their minds more often, but conversation ceased.

The major differences between early warning signals and serious warning signals are the depth and duration of unhappy feelings. In the early stages, feelings become intense over issues but recede often, to return again. In the serious warning stage, unhappy feelings become almost continuing, affecting the individuals and the relationship adversely day in and day out.

By the time a relationship is in trouble to the point of serious warnings, anger, recognized or not, is being manifested to such an extent that even the smallest incident is magnified, and there has been such a severe breakdown in communications between the partners that one or both may find that they are avoiding communication entirely. You may have a feeling that it just isn't worth your time and effort to communicate, because nothing will be accomplished anyway, or because past attempts to discuss a problem have ended in so much unpleasantness and hurt for either or both of you.

The one word that applies to all the serious warning signals is *isolation,* either self-imposed or imposed by the unavailability of the other.

We have identified seven serious warning signals.

1. Complete breakdown of communication but attempts to improve things by working independently of each other
2. Attacks on each other's integrity
3. Withdrawal
4. Lack of self-worth
5. Looking outside the marriage for consolation
6. Giving up
7. Ambivalence

IS THERE ANYTHING I CAN DO?—Independent Efforts

The major characteristic of this signal is that a decision is made by one person and not by the two together. A partner who is hoping to save a relationship may avoid verbal or direct communication because there never seems to be a good time to bring up problems or discuss feelings, or may decide that the resulting "bad scene" will do more harm than good. When one partner or both think that the other will not respond and when promises have been made and broken repeatedly, feelings of anger, confusion, frustration, and resentment build up to the point that one more unpleasant scene is not worth the effort. You may realize that something is seriously wrong with your relationship, but because of a severe lack of communication, you may not know what it is. You may try in many ways to correct what you feel may be the problem but may mislead yourself, because you are cut off from your partner's point of view, which creates new problems.

Often one or both partners may attempt to ease marital stress by absorbing themselves in projects independent of each other.

Men may take on an additional load at work, often involving more travel. Women may become more absorbed in the children and/or time spent with other women, especially those who are divorced. Both may spend excessive time with community jobs. Many couples will go in debt to buy a second car or a larger house or all those things they feel will lead to happiness for everyone. For instance, the couple may take an expensive vacation they really can't afford and may have a wonderful time while they are away, only to find upon returning that nothing has changed and problems have not been solved. Many times, a vacation can be a real boost to a relationship, giving the couple needed time away from the day-to-day responsibilities of home and job and a chance for partners to devote themselves to each other. However, serious problems will not be solved and partners may feel somewhat perplexed when they return to find that their relationship has not improved. One husband remarked, "I took her everywhere she wanted to go, spent all that money, and nothing has changed." The wife remarked, "He's a different person out of town, but once we were home everything was just like it used to be."

Sometimes one or both of the partners may launch a self-improvement campaign, feeling that now they really will stick to that diet, get more exercise, or try to be more interesting. A wife may try to show more interest in her husband's work, devote more time to keeping a spotless house, have the children quiet and a drink waiting when he arrives home, or cook his favorite foods and serve them by candlelight. She may also make herself more available sexually in an attempt to bridge the communication gap.

A husband may suddenly launch a real clean-up, paint-up, fix-up campaign, or become overly attentive, bringing his wife presents, taking her out more often, or waiting on her both at home and in a group of friends.

All these are examples of positive attempts at grasping for something to help the deteriorating relationship. The partner making these attempts is usually well aware that the situation is pretty serious and may be frightened by the thought of total separation and divorce. The attempts may temporarily relieve the situation, but they do not ultimately solve any problems. In fact, if only one partner is making the effort, even more intense feelings of resentment and lack of support may build up. Eventually a martyred feeling may intensify. "I do everything and no one else does anything," or "I'm the only one making any effort and I'm tired of getting nowhere." Then anger and despair build up to compound the problem.

GOTCHA—Attacking Integrity

When frustration with a partner has become a consistent feeling, and direct, positive communication is gone, attacks on each other's integrity will ensue. Lack of communication is so devastating to us that we may want to shake the other into any response, even if it is fighting, verbally or physically. We may wish to inflict emotional wounds as deep as our own.

Attacking can be done subtly or overtly. It can be done in private or in public, verbally or nonverbally. The effect depends largely on the context and the feelings involved. For example, "Harry's all thumbs" may be a personal private joke at home, but this statement might humiliate him if publicly voiced. Sue might not enjoy cooking, but for her husband constantly to report in public that she is "no cook" can become serious.

Attacks can be aimed at the sexuality, appearance, achievements, intentions, and efforts of the other. Sex can be a tremendous weapon. A wife may withhold sex, using intimidation to emasculate her husband. A husband can punish in the same manner. Both may ignore the other's good qualities and accomplishments by belittling to the point of almost nonexistence.

Verbal attacks can be direct or fielded through children or outsiders. "He doesn't know what he is talking about." "You ought to see the house when I get home; it's unbelievable!" Or: "Don't mind old George. He's in male menopause; hence, the sports car and jazzy clothes."

I CAN TAKE CARE OF MYSELF—Withdrawal

Images of a perfect relationship with a new partner can be harbored to be brought out and played with in times of deep stress. Unhappy fantasies or death wishes for the other person can surface, making the partner wonder about his own emotional stability. When a husband is late from work his wife might start anticipating a fatal accident. When he drives in, she may experience feelings of anger toward him and horror at her own emotions. "But wouldn't it be a nice tidy way to clean up the whole mess!"

A husband might sit in a chair quietly watching his wife, thinking up as many ways as possible to do her in. In the long run, he won't feel too good about himself either.

Another form of fantasy that can be easily changed into reality is an attempt by one partner to make the other take action toward a divorce. "I haven't got the guts, but I'll make her so miserable that she will have to end this thing." However, when the issue of divorce is brought up, either or both might become so frightened at the thought of total rejection or the possibility of living alone that they retreat hastily back into the fantasy world and all the old patterns.

Sometimes sudden and unrealistic changes in attitude take place when we become entirely self-motivated and may in fact have no positive feelings left for the other partner or may be so angry that we feel we will just show the other partner that he or she really isn't needed. One wife, who really didn't want a divorce, told her husband that she wanted a legal separation because she felt that she could manage the home and children better by herself. The wife secretly hoped that this would force the husband to accept more responsibility, when, in fact, it was the beginning of the end. They divorced three years later, and the wife was forced to put her statement into practice. Euphoria over the feeling, "I can make it on my own," didn't last very long.

The need to pleasure oneself at the expense of the other partner or the entire family is viewed by all as an act of pure selfishness. Both husbands and wives have been guilty of this. One husband bought a sports car, boat, and joined a country club, all for his own pleasure. This forced the wife to juggle her household budget to meet necessary basic expenses. Needless to say, this only added kindling to the fire. The husband could not really enjoy his new pleasures, and the wife's resentment continued to mount. Wives have been guilty of charging items for their personal pleasure at local stores to such an amount that their husbands have been forced to suffer the embarrassment of serving public notice that they will no longer be responsible for their wives' bills. Wives have also been known to spend the grocery money on themselves at the expense of the entire family. The husband or wife who retaliates by meeting his or her own needs and desires with total lack of regard for the other partner is only adding to the problems of a relationship already in serious trouble.

WHAT'S WRONG WITH ME?—Lack of Self-Worth

Many times, when you are involved in a troubled relationship, while not knowing the real problem, you may begin to feel that you are becoming a different person.

The usually calm, easygoing, capable person may find himself upset by almost every little thing. To his own horror, he is throwing things, screaming at partner and children, crying over small unimportant incidents, and always "on edge." One husband said that he knew things were pretty bad when he shoved his wife, knocking her to the floor. He was appalled at what he had done and frightened that he had expressed his anger so violently. Perhaps this is an attempt to make the other person respond in some fashion or to deliberately inflict hurt. Whichever is the reason, he may wonder, "What's wrong with me?"

For others, there may be a conflict in a person's behavior at home and in public. There is still the need to have the "outside world" see everything as near-perfect. "After all, if I'm married to this person, I don't want everyone to think he is all bad." If one of the partners feels embarrassment over the behavior of the other partner, they may find themselves publicly covering up or making excuses. A husband or wife who drinks excessively in public may become flirty and cause out-of-place, unfavorable scenes, even if only by conversation. The embarrassed partner is always finding some excuse to go home or to turn down invitations from the beginning. A partner who misbehaves may realize later that she is unpleasant to be around and usually will have a feeling of "What's wrong with me?" or "I don't like what I do, but I can't seem to help it." A husband or wife may make a phone call to the hostess the day after the incident to relay an apology.

Even if anger over the behavior of the other partner is well covered up in public, it is usually vented in some way once the couple are within the walls of their own home. This may take the form of screaming, physically harming the other person, withdrawing sex, or just giving them the silent treatment—not even a "good night." This only reinforces "What's wrong with me?"

Sometimes anger is manifested in the form of severe physical pain in the lower back, abdomen, or head, and it is not unusual that a person may develop insomnia. An examination by a doctor often shows no physical cause for the discomfort. Medication, while bringing relief, does not cure the cause. No one can exist on "uppers" and "downers" forever. This rubber band syndrome, under which a person is continuously flexed between emotional extremes, will reduce resiliency and ability to function.

Many times you may be extremely tired and feel so depressed that you lose all desire to do the things you would normally enjoy. The feeling that "Nothing will get any better no matter what I do" seems to overcome any motivation to try to make things better even for only one day. When anger is manifested in this way, it causes you to have a feeling of helplessness and uselessness—not seeming to be able to do anything about the situation and at the same time being unhappy with the knowledge that you are probably causing those close to you just as much unhappiness.

A person locked into deep depression may often feel that suicide is the only answer to the problem. You may feel that you can't seem to correct the situation or find an answer to "What's wrong with me?" You feel that if you were no longer around, all concerned would be better off. You may in fact have lost all motivation or desire to face anyone or any situation. A partner may threaten suicide by telling the other that he just can't make it on his own, or by expressing the feeling that she will be completely destroyed by divorce. This person is begging for help and support but may find that the threats only serve to cause the other partner to be even more disgusted and alienated.

Often the partner dealing with suicidal tendencies no longer has the desire to be around the spouse. He just wants to "stop the world and get off" and feels a real desperation to have time alone and especially time away from his partner. When verbal communication has virtually disintegrated, neither partner really cares about being at home when the other partner is, or if they are at home together, they get involved in anything and everything that will exclude the other. The wife may see to it that she is busy with evening meetings of one kind or another, or the husband may suddenly have to work late every evening at the office. One or both may seek relief by frequenting local bars or drinking at home, until they really aren't aware of anything going on, allowing this state of induced euphoria to insulate them from unpleasant confrontations.

Often anger and lack of self-worth manifested in these ways may affect relationships with others or even productiveness at work. A person who is always uptight, tired, or bitchy is not a pleasant person to be around, whether it be spouse, children, family, friends, or business associates. Subsequently, a real feeling of despair and "What's wrong with me?" may be further strengthened.

SOMEBODY HELP!
MAKE ME FEEL BETTER!—Looking Outside

When one partner is not meeting the needs of the other it is not unusual that someone outside the relationship is sought for comfort and needed advice. A wife may depend on male members of her family or a trusted male friend for help with jobs around the house or for advice in other areas. A husband may bend the ear of a trusted male or female friend to give him understanding and support by just listening. Seeking relief from someone outside the relationship usually only adds to feelings of inadequacy and heightens resentment and feelings of anger on the part of the other partner.

Sometimes one or both of the partners may resort to an affair as a means to relieve their misery, or to reassure themselves of their worth. They may feel that an affair will be a boost to their marriage by proving that they can still have a meaningful relationship with a member of the opposite sex and therefore give them more confidence in seeking a renewed relationship with their spouse. There may be the feeling that "if someone else finds me attractive, surely my spouse will wake up to what he has at home." An affair may be taken as a sign "that nothing is wrong with me, so it must be my spouse." Sometimes, though, a partner in a miserable relationship may be simply and desperately in need of an ego boost or a way out.

The reasons for an affair can be wide and varied. Persons who have become extremely lonely in the marriage may long for a kind word or a warm touch. However, one thing may lead to another and they may find themselves far more involved than had been intended. An affair also may be sought because of fear. A partner may feel that she is losing what she has and cannot face the prospect of being alone, so she finds someone else to meet her needs and relieve her feelings of rejection. Seeking out an affair indicates that there is a serious problem with the marriage. An affair may at best bring the couple to the point of facing their problems or at least finding out where they are in their relationship. However, in the end all who are involved suffer some form of hurt and one or both of the partners may not be willing to live with the situation afterward.

THIS TIME I'VE HAD IT—Giving·Up

Periodically something might occur that will cause a person to throw in the towel. "I've had it!" "I'll never do anything for that S.O.B. again." "I want an out." "I want peace." "She is the world's worst bitch." Then fear of the unknown, concern over the children, and even concern for the other partner will surface, turning the relationship back to its old rut. This can continue for years, or forever, especially if your partner apologizes and promises that "it won't happen again." You want to believe your spouse, so you hang in there for another round, hoping each time that promises will be kept.

I DON'T KNOW WHAT I WANT—Ambivalence

By this time, a pattern of total confusion has been established. An individual or both partners find themselves living in a jungle of radically swinging emotions, involving all the warning signals mentioned. They are no longer in or out of the relationship. They are not committed to its continuing or to its end. Confusion reigns and a feeling of absolute helplessness and despair overpowers them. They are victims of circumstances that will continue forever unless they choose to do something responsible about their situation.

POSITIVE ACTION

If one or both partners become so totally miserable that they recognize the need for action, they will then make an attempt to restore their lives. Often the final thrust leading to the decision to proceed with the divorce can seemingly be very small, like the straw that broke the camel's back. The real problem or problems can be different or very similar, but the feelings are usually the same in all troubled relationships. Once one of the partners realizes that a serious problem is the real reason behind their feelings of anger, disappointment, depression, confusion, despair, resentment, rejection, or frustration, they will begin to take some action.

Up until this point, attempts have been made in some form to revive the situation, which by now has become miserable. One or both of the partners have reacted in their own way and still may not know what the real problem is. If these serious warnings are ignored or cannot be corrected, the marriage will move into the decision-making stage. However, even a relationship this deeply in trouble can sometimes be reclaimed with the help of a professional, provided each partner has a genuine desire and willingness to try to save the marriage. If the marriage cannot be saved, the help of a qualified, unbiased, uninvolved person can help the couple through the decision-making prior to divorce, and on to an acceptance of the situation afterward.

HOMEWORK

1. Sit down, with some "protected" time.
2. Ask yourself if you have moved from early to serious warning signals. How much and how long ago?
3. Do you *want* to do anything about it?
4. Find a way to consult your partner. If a face-to-face talk won't work, write a letter or telephone.
5. See and talk honestly with a mental health professional (psychiatrist, psychologist, social worker, minister). Make sure that you are comfortable with that person and that you get a sense of assurance and caring. It's best to try another professional if you don't feel able to trust him or her.

CHAPTER 3

Money and Marriage

It is not possible for most people to have all they want. Therefore, when choices have to be made about what is purchased, there is certain conflict. Many writers in the field of counseling say that conflict over money has risen to the forefront as a presenting cause in marital discord. "I work hard, and she spends the money." "He thinks that because his work gets the paycheck, I have just been sitting around all day." Those are common "openers" with a dissatisfied couple in a counselor's office.

But the issue isn't really money in most cases. The real issue is values. Each of us has been raised with our own unique value system about what in life is worthwhile. Where do we "invest" ourselves and our energy for the greatest return? There are a lot of places calling for that investment of ourselves and, inevitably, our money. Thus, the differences begin to arise. How we want to spend our money tells us a great deal about our philosophy of life, our concept of human nature, and even whether we are hopeful or despairing about life.

For instance, one partner wants to save money for either a dream vacation or an emergency nest egg. The other partner wants to spend the money when it is earned. Considerable disagreements can take place on that issue. That first partner may always have placed a great deal of emphasis in life on having something to look forward to. The present is made more rich by the promise of something coming. The other partner has learned that if you don't enjoy what you have now, you may lose it. We have here two very different value systems.

In another situation, a major dispute takes place about getting counseling. One partner wants to spend the money on the belief that change really can take place in a person's life. That is an optimism about the capacity of human nature to change. The other partner considers the investment a waste of time, because you "can't change people." The argument may be stated as being over money, but the conflict is really over two very different concepts of human nature.

There are as many degrees of seriousness and intensity to the problem as there are couples. It can range from one minor incident or misunderstanding to the extreme of the partners having opposite value systems from which they are operating. One couple's difficulty over money might be discussed and resolved simply and satisfactorily, while another couple may spend their entire married life rehashing the same point and effecting no solution because of uncompromising value systems and/or human nature. The real key to resolving many arguments over money is to try to stop long enough to look under the argument. What is really at stake in this controversy?

One couple held regularly recurring arguments every year at the time the income tax refund check came. Steve wanted to put the money into a prepaid mortgage payment account to get them ahead on their house payments. He presented a sophisticated case, being a lawyer, about the good sense of forestalling future difficulties if a financial collapse came by having the house paid off early. Nancy was quite adamant about putting the money into a savings account, arguing that it would be available in case of emergency and would earn interest. Some exploration underneath that argument revealed that her family, when she was growing up, had had several occasions of hard times because of a frivolous father who never had a backlog of money. She had vowed to provide herself with more security by building up a nest egg. Steve, on the other hand, had been taught the importance of not letting money sit idle. To do so was irresponsible if there were unpaid bills to cover, and one should work constantly toward eliminating outstanding debts. The discovery of these emotional factors, or "values," lying underneath their ritualistic argument didn't make the feelings go away, but it certainly led to more understanding in arriving at a compromise that took these needs and values more seriously.

Let us look at some examples of the types of money problems evident in marriages. Note that most have an underlying issue and require careful examination by both partners "to see it for what it really is." In applying the same examples to different couples, one sees that the underlying issues can vary greatly from couple to couple.

We often find both partners working at the time of marriage. When the couple are young and have only each other to be responsible for, the first strains over money are not taken too seriously. It is fun and challenging to begin to furnish an apartment, accumulate belongings, and start a family. Usually this is done without any decided budget, but just living from paycheck to paycheck. When things get really tight with incoming bills or unexpected expenses, the couple ease up, catch up, then begin to spend again. When this situation repeats itself enough, some couples will work out a budget so they will have a more consistent and workable spending pattern. A budget is practical but not a manageable approach for all couples. Through sheer trial and error couples must work this out for themselves. Help from a counselor and/or banker could be valuable for a couple interested in using a budget but having little or no experience in setting up one.

Whether there is a budget or not, usually one partner takes the responsibility of paying the bills. It is wise for both partners to be apprised of the checkbook's standing on a regular basis, so that neither thinks that a sudden expense can be withstood just because things *seem* to be going along so well.

The "surprise," when it falls in the category of overspending, is a unique experience and one of the most difficult and touchy situations to handle. If a couple are on a minimum income, each dollar is usually accounted for in a month's normal expenses. Jean comes home with a new sweater for Jim. It wasn't planned for, and it's going to necessitate juggling the finances to make necessary payments. Jean is very pleased that she was so thoughtful to get a "surprise" for her husband. She hasn't really considered how or when it's going to be paid for, but "it's the thought that counts," after all. Jim's reaction is one of appreciation for the gift but concern over the cost and paying for it. He has always managed the checkbook well, and Jean feels he can handle this. Jim suggests returning the sweater, and Jean is crushed and says he's taking all the enjoyment out of giving. He says he'll keep the sweater and juggle next month's expenses to pay for it. Jean is elated, but Jim secretly is building up resentment for having to revise payments on existing charges, and he feels that Jean has actually been selfish in the long run. Inwardly, he feels it was for her own satisfaction that she made the purchase, with little thought of its wide-range effects.

This may not happen on a consistent basis, but along with other money problems, it can cause ill feelings to mount to a volcanic stage. It's dangerous, so be aware!

One of the most abused approaches to spending revolves around the use of credit cards. For most people, obtaining credit is easy, and often credit cards are sent without application. For business and practical purposes, a certain amount of credit should be established. If a credit card is temperately used, it truly can be a convenience instead of a continual burden. However, some persons use credit as if a purchase will never have to be paid for and are unable to see the long-range effect. Some view credit as an outlet for their impatience and are willing to worry later about paying, no matter how financially strapped they become. Excessive use of credit cards and high interest rates cause some people to get so deep in debt that often the next step is to secure a consolidation loan. This is a vicious circle and one that can contribute toward family and financial failure. Don't get addicted; it is a costly habit.

Just as overspending can be a problem, being "tight" can cause a marriage to be strained. If both partners are of the nature to be tight, then there probably won't be a problem. But if one is, and one is not, there is likely to be discord. One may feel cheated, unloved, unappreciated, and untrusted. It is a problem that well may require professional help to find a solution, lest dissolution of the marriage occur.

When both partners work, there is the natural feeling of "What do I deserve and get for bringing in income?" Susan and Don both work full time, and she is planning to buy new clothes in the spring with money she has saved during the winter. Don comes home announcing that he has bought a one-third interest in a boat and will need all their savings for his portion of the investment. An argument follows, with Susan expressing that she isn't interested in the boat, so why should her savings go toward the payment, and Don stating he wanted the boat to provide entertainment for them both and he couldn't back out on the other partners. Susan feels that she is being taken advantage of and reaping little or no benefit from "her own income." Don feels she isn't appreciative of his effort for their mutual benefit and pleasure. Both feel that the other is being selfish.

Discussions on major expenditures beforehand are helpful in avoiding arguments over money. Overspending on one person's part while the other is left to juggle expenses is unfair, frustrating, and a dangerous threat to a marriage, if such action continues and is allowed to go unchecked.

Then too, there may be no question that each *deserves* direct enjoyment from money he or she alone earns. But deserving is one thing; being able to afford is another. Dave has worked overtime in order to earn extra income for new golf clubs. He has almost enough saved when his wife becomes ill and has an emergency operation. Even with their hospitalization insurance, Dave must use all his savings to help pay the medical expenses. There is no question that he has worked hard and deserves the new golf clubs, but circumstances are such that he cannot afford them now. There is a happy medium between "deserving something" and being able to afford it, and this must be found by each couple.

One of the most vicious money problems comes when there is a need to "keep up with the Joneses." This is particularly bad when only one partner has this desire. If there is serious intent on this status climb, the marriage is certain to be affected negatively. The strain emotionally and financially in the effort to "keep up with the Joneses" can become almost unbearable. Betty is obsessed with having as much as her neighbor and is constantly needling Bob to get this and that and often makes major purchases without his consent. Bob is resentful that practically all he has earned goes for these things, and Betty and Bob fight constantly over this. For

Betty it is an insatiable appetite, because there will always be someone with more than she has. Bob will be subjected to the incessant purchasing unless they can work out a more compatible arrangement.

Actually, if *both* partners want to "keep up with the Joneses," there is usually little or no arguing. Though they may never have any savings and be paying on time for nearly everything, they are both working together satisfactorily.

Another problem over money exists when one partner refuses to take an interest or deal with the finances. This was experienced by Jo Ann when Sam "threw up his hands" over their purchasing a new home. The investment was good; the price was right, and she was attempting to stimulate interest in Sam. Their family had grown, and a new house was needed. Jo Ann was a prudent shopper and a good businesswoman but did want help in making the decision and discussion on the best way to finance the purchase. She felt completely alone in her efforts and knew from experience that if the house were bought, the first thing to go wrong would be thrown back in her face with a "Well, that's what you wanted; you handled it." She felt she was being given no support, help, or consideration. This had happened before in other circumstances, and it was no fun going it alone and having to accept full responsibility.

Agreeing to priorities can be the first hurdle in this "money game." This is why having a mutual value system, or at least compatible ones, plays such an important role in the couple's lives. If there is a serious division over priorities, and this is never worked through, divorce may come about as a direct result. A wife may see saving for a house or new clothes as a major priority and be unable to understand her husband's desire for a sports car and sporting equipment as of major importance to him. They may agree on saving for a house and yet disagree on secondary priorities. Consequently, the husband may come home with new sporting equipment for himself at the same time the wife has updated her wardrobe. The result is the same—another argument over who is spending too much money on "unnecessary" things.

Many couples do not take seriously enough their *initial* money problems. One may simply resign oneself to having constant dissension over money. Fights may occur, with no solution or compromise; living and spending goes on; and the problem gets more and more serious, without the couple's ever realizing how much the marriage is really being affected. After all, they love each other, and money matters don't seem likely to get to the proportion of seriously affecting their feelings for each other. They remember saying the words "for richer, for poorer" and maybe the money problems are just part of the package of marriage.

The most important characteristic for financial compatibility in a marriage is that of trust. When this exists, major problems of overspending and tightness are virtually nonexistent. A woman working full time can feel some freedom with her income, and the husband doesn't live in fear of not making ends meet.

In attempting to work successfully through financial problems, couples should first be aware that a problem exists. They should take it seriously and not harbor bad feelings. If, after you admit that a problem exists, discussion and efforts between you and your partner do not prove helpful, then seek the help of a professional counselor and/or banker. If a budget is your approach, try making it fun by having penalties and rewards worked into the rules. Communicate on priorities, adjustments to them as time goes on, schedule of payments, savings, increases in insurance premiums, and unexpected expenses. Decide what are major expenditures for your family and discuss before making these purchases. But by all means, communicate. Money problems can do damage, possibly "costing" you your marriage.

CHAPTER 4

Sex and Marriage

Second only to money, sex is a frequent presenting complaint in marital relationships. While money primarily seems to highlight the value conflicts in a relationship, sex seems to highlight the differences in needs for intimacy and sharing.

Just as with money, there is a plethora of books on the market about how to cure your sexual difficulties through the use of this or that technique or gadget. The expectations that many writers throw at you in terms of what a sexual relationship should be would test Don Juan himself. Just that kind of romantic idealism has often created dissatisfaction in many marriages.

Let's back up and examine the issue more carefully. First, lack of satisfaction in the sexual arena of marriage may be caused by some sort of physical problem. Therefore, if there is difficulty, a good physical examination is in order for both partners, including open discussion with the physician about what the problem is. More often than not, the problem is not physical, but it is best that you eliminate that possibility at the first, so you do not painfully go through all kinds of therapy only to discover that the problem could have been remedied long ago.

The second important issue is that sex is more than intercourse. Sexuality is almost as broad a matter as you can imagine. The exchange of affection, the greetings and farewells each day, the willingness to sit close and talk, the touches that are given and received at a party or in the kitchen—all these things and more are sexual. And they affect the act of intercourse itself. Is intercourse simply a "physical thing"? Or is it an even more intimate and fulfilling expression of all those things mentioned above? Much of the literature on sex seems to indicate that the richness of intercourse itself is very much a product of the richness of all those other kinds of exchanges that have preceded it. And, often, when intercourse has not been fulfilling, the improvement of communication in other areas results in more richness in the marital bed as well.

So, a problem with sex is a problem with communication in many cases. This means that communication should be open in all areas of the relationship. John and Mary had come to a counselor because of regular disagreements about the frequency of John's sexual demands. She found it repulsive that he wanted intercourse nightly. After a survey of the rest of their relationship, it became quite clear that they were engaged in a very self-defeating kind of situation. By the end of the day they were both quite tired. He, in fear that she would go to bed and go to sleep early, would begin propositioning her from the moment that he came in the door. She, in anticipation of his amorous moves, would spend a good part of the day dreading it and would be angry as soon as he came in. The conflict would reach a crescendo in terms of loud shouting and following each other around the house. The ending would vary in terms of what happened physically. Some nights she would give in, letting him know quite clearly that it was *his* idea. Other nights she would refuse but be resentful and guilty that she did not feel more willing to meet his announced needs. He, on the other hand, would maintain an angry and martyrish attitude about either situation, giving neither himself nor her any relief.

Over a period of several weeks the nightly ritual was changed. It was agreed that they would not discuss sex for a while. Upon reuniting each evening they would sit down, discuss each other's activities during the day, read or watch television together, talk over any decisions that had to be made, exchange less erotic physical affection, and otherwise move through the evening without the pressure of anticipating "when the battle would start." After a time, they began to enjoy each other sexually in the full sense of the word, that is, they found that the entire evening had been a time of enjoying each other. Disagreements? Certainly. But, they didn't all revolve around intercourse. Soon, intercourse was enjoyable to both, and the frequency was more acceptable to both. He found that the relationship was satisfactory enough that intercourse was not necessary every night in order to assure that the relationship was still intact. She found that intercourse was more attractive because it was not pushed. A common situation? Only in that resolution of other factors led to a fairly natural solution of the original focus of their conflict.

Other couples cope with varying problems. A wife complaining that her husband doesn't satisfy her sexually, a husband "just never getting around to it"—all illustrate a lack of full understanding about sexuality. Sex is not something we do *to* or *for* each other. It is something partners do *with* each other, and each must take equal responsibility. A continuing unresolved conflict elsewhere can put a damper on sexual desire.

Another issue involved with sex in marriage still centers in the area of communication, but this time it is even more specific. Stated simply, it is very important that the partners tell each other, specifically and out loud, what they like and do not like about sex. There is still a prevalent myth in our society that a man is "supposed to know" how to make a woman sexually happy. There is also a myth that a woman is "not supposed" to tell a man "how to do it." Fortunately, those myths are going by the boards, thanks to much research done by such persons as Masters and Johnson.

It is very important that the partners tell each other what is pleasing and what is not pleasing, not only in intercourse but also in exchanges of affection generally. With all the literature circulating these days about the "normality" of different procedures, it is all too often the case that one mate will read about it and then "assume" that the other mate has been waiting breathlessly to try it. The result is often a spontaneous attempt, rejection, and bad feelings never discussed later. Saying "Let's try_____" doesn't burst the romantic balloon. In fact, it can make the experiment more fun by virtue of both partners being involved. Or, if one partner doesn't feel ready to try that particular method, then interruption of a pleasurable experience doesn't have to take place.

Talk with each other about what you would like to try. Just as important, talk about what you do not want to try. Try the technique known as "pleasuring." Both partners, having agreed, disrobe. One lies still and is the "recipient." The other partner strokes, caresses, and otherwise "pleasures," the mate with the understanding that the objective is not intercourse but pleasurable sensations. The "recipient" tells the other partner what is liked and what is disliked. The roles are then reversed. The objective is to "get to know" each other's preferences with regard to physical affection. The same kind of experimentation should go on in the areas of wearing apparel, smells (perfumes, shaving cologne, etc.), hair styles, etc. The more you talk, the more you know. And the more you know, the more you can give to each other.

That leads to a fourth area, giving. All too often marital partners start keeping score in the matter of sex. If I didn't get fully satisfied last time, then it's my turn tonight. If that dynamic becomes very frequent, the result is two free agents out for all they can *get.* The result is lack of satisfaction on the part of both and a guarantee of some anger next time. The purpose of learning about each other's preferences is to be able to *give* more effectively. Another myth in our culture is that one mate is responsible for whether the other mate reaches orgasm or not. That is not true. What is true, however, is that the one partner should be willing to be responsive to what the other partner asks as they reach toward orgasm. The distinction may seem subtle, but it is true. If you feel responsible for the other's satisfaction, there will be some bad moments. But if you feel willing to *assist* the other partner, there can be more joy on the part of both at having achieved a good experience *together.* And, by the way, you don't have to plan out the whole experience in advance. It's fair, and helpful, to talk about what you want and need during the experience itself. Again, it doesn't de-romanticize things. It helps.

In many cases there are various psychological or technical causes for a lack of satisfaction in the experiences of sex and intercourse. There are also specific techniques that can be used to remedy them. Such problems are best dealt with in a professional setting and not in this book. It is certainly worth your time and energy to get help.

The purpose of this chapter has been to point out in a summary way the various kinds of issues that can affect the sexual relationship within a marriage. Difficulty is not a signal of divorce. It is a signal, again, of some things that need to be dealt with directly, rather than passively. Talk about sex with your partner. Ask if he or she is satisfied. Say whether you are. Tell your partner what is fulfilling to you and what is not. Enjoy this deeply enriching aspect of your marriage which is to be carried out according to your preferences and with your frequency and not by anybody else's.

CHAPTER 5

Divorce and the Church

There are a great many questions concerning the church and its attitude toward the divorced. Enough sermons have been preached and scornful looks given to make those considering divorce wonder about their position and their welcome. This chapter is intended to speak directly to the concerns that many churches have about ministry to the divorced. It also offers an interpretation of Biblical passages, for there are many divorced persons who carry a sense of guilt and shame from a religious frame of reference about their decision.

There can be no doubt that the New Testament is very clear in its attitude on the matter. The Gospel of Mark, which is commonly regarded as the earliest written account of the life of Jesus, doesn't hedge.

> And Pharisees came up and in order to test him asked, "Is it lawful for a man to divorce his wife?" He answered them, "What did Moses command you?" They said, "Moses allowed a man to write a certificate of divorce, and to put her away." But Jesus said to them, "For your hardness of heart he wrote you this commandment. But from the beginning of creation, 'God made them male and female.' 'For this reason a man shall leave his father and mother and be joined to his wife, and the two shall become one flesh.' So they are no longer two but one flesh. What therefore God has joined together, let not man put asunder."
>
> And in the house the disciples asked him again about this matter. And he said to them, "Whoever divorces his wife and marries another,

commits adultery against her; and if she divorces her husband and marries another, she commits adultery." (Mark 10:2–12)

There can be no doubt from such a passage that Jesus believed deeply that marriage should be viewed as a permanent relationship. He drew an indisputably clear picture of the intention of that state as God intended it.

In Matthew, which was probably written later, Jesus is quoted again on the matter:

> It was also said, "Whoever divorces his wife, let him give her a certificate of divorce." But I say to you that every one who divorces his wife, except on the ground of unchastity, makes her an adulteress; and whoever marries a divorced woman commits adultery. (Matt. 5:31–32)

The view is just as clear here. However, one ground for divorce has been introduced. Many scholars feel that Matthew's account represents a mellowing that was going on in the early church. Apparently the church began to wrestle with the realism of adhering to an absolute position as stated in Mark. It seemed to recognize the need for exceptions because of human frailty. Nevertheless, the Scripture still is quite clear about the premium placed on the intention of permanence in marriage.

With that principle of permanence stated so clearly, we can now talk about a view of divorce in the church today. Jesus was stating in unambiguous fashion the importance of marriage as a permanent, stabilizing relationship in life. Life, if lived as God intended, would have no divorce. When a marriage dissolves, whatever the reason, it is not ever to be taken lightly. A divorce is indisputably a failure to live up to the expectations of the New Testament. It is a result of sin, which means literally "to fall short of the mark." When two people divorce, they have indeed fallen short of the mark; they have been less than they had hoped in their relationship, and certainly less than God hopes. This knowledge should play a part in the process of your decision-making. It makes choosing to divorce a very heavy decision. Anyone who enters into marriage or divorce with less than a serious attitude about the issues involved has indeed "fallen short of the mark." In summary, the church views divorce with a very critical eye toward the motives involved.

In addition to the seriousness of such decisions, it is important also to recognize the promise of forgiveness presented in the New Testament. One doesn't find any unpardonable sins there. There is always the promise of forgiveness, hinging on the repentance of the sinner. Forgiveness implies that there needs to be a prior judgment of one's own actions—in this case, failure. A person considering divorce needs to take fully into account all the factors of the situation. You have to be honest about your shortcomings and how you contributed to the failure of your marriage. This kind of self-honesty is a form of repentance. Once that is done and a decision made, that doesn't make the decision "right." Who can say whether a decision like that is "right"? This does mean that a person can move on in life with a sense of integrity, having experienced self-honesty and recognizing the need for forgiveness.

The theology of the New Testament is really telling us something that long preceded formal psychology. When we break off a relationship without carefully weighing the implications and consequences, the odds are that we will bear varying degrees of guilt, grief, depression, wondering, etc., for a long time. There are far too many cases in which that is exactly what happens. The years are followed by an inability to trust members of the opposite sex, confusing anger, a cynical outlook on life, and a myriad of other crippling emotions. The New Testament teaches us to acknowledge our mistakes with all the pain that may ensue, so that we can move on, knowing that we are "forgiven."

What, then, can the church do? In our case, after some individual counseling of varying lengths of time, the support group for divorced persons was created. The purpose of our group was not to provide "therapy" per se. Nor was it a chance to criticize the missing ex-partner. It was an opportunity to "confess" where things went wrong, to examine feelings, to admit to personal failings, to study the process that had taken place so that it wouldn't be repeated, and to make decisions about the future. Children were discussed. Jobs were discussed. Dating was discussed. By sponsoring this group, the church provided opportunities for reconciliation, perhaps not of the broken marriages but with the future and with oneself.

If a church says there is no room for divorced persons because they are wrong, there is a painful absence of the New Testament emphasis on forgiveness. On the other hand, if there is a blissful, passive, unconcerned acceptance of divorced persons, there is an equally painful absence of caring enough to encourage growth.

The church is charged with the responsibility of inviting back into the home those who may feel "exiled." That seems to be done best when there is a firm and tender invitation to face one's difficulties and be made whole. Then each can minister to the other, because we all have shortcomings to be admitted and shared.

If you are wrestling with a decision to divorce, or if you are experiencing some of those early warning signals, or if you are experiencing the turmoil that follows the decision and the action of divorce, seek out the counsel of a church that seems to offer that difficult balance between judgment and forgiveness. It doesn't have to be the minister. It may well be a group such as ours. But take advantage of it. You deserve it.

CHAPTER 6

Decision-Making

In making a decision concerning divorce, one must consider many choices and alternatives. This chapter will offer these as well as an outline of the process of decision-making. On paper it may look easy and pat. It isn't. We recognize completely that your thoughts and emotions will jump from one alternative to another and back again. Feelings are confused. A decision may be made, later changed and reconsidered.

The process of making the decision to end a marriage, or to try to change it, or to accept it as it is, is a long, agonizing experience.

When a relationship has existed in the serious warning signals stage for any length of time, you are not likely to be committed to either the marriage or a divorce, but usually exist in an ambivalent state which creates a desperate feeling of helplessness. "This is the way it's going to be." "I can't change things."

WHO IS TO MAKE THIS DECISION?

Choosing to be the decision maker is an uncomfortable step. Often couples will hand the responsibility back and forth, each hoping the other will take the initiative. Sometimes a partner may even live a life of actions, hoping to force the other into divorce. This can go on for years and is usually unproductive. One must finally give serious consideration to making the decision.

Eventually something will happen that will trigger one or both into an awareness that "something must be done." It could be an event. One person sought professional help as the result of deep concern over a child. The conclusion of the first interview with a psychologist was that nothing could be done to help the child until the marriage was straightened out, either through commitment to the marriage or divorce. It became immediately apparent that a decision *had* to be made for the health of the family. A tremendous sense of relief was experienced, with a feeling that "at last something would be resolved." Another event might be a job change that requires the family to relocate. This will force the partners to look closely at their problems. It may be something as small as the lack of support over household chores, or thorough disgust with the partner or oneself. If the feeling "I can't stand it" evolves and remains consistent, a person may act. "I can't stand it" can mean "I can't stand myself." A person who prefers to feel good about himself or herself will not usually allow this to endure and will eventually act.

There seem to be three choices at this stage:

1. To grit one's teeth and plunge into divorce, perhaps talking with only one's friends and family
2. To look actively for a new person to use as a crutch to help bridge the gap of loneliness, to restore loss of self-esteem and ego—in other words, an affair
3. To seek professional help, either as a couple or an individual

I CAN DO ANYTHING . . . ALL BY MYSELF—To Plunge

Going it alone, without the aid of a reliable professional, is not recommended. An honest understanding of what has happened to the relationship is essential to ensure your healthy future. Talking with friends and family will not help you get to the essence of the trouble. Family and friends are just that. More than likely they will "side" with the troubled partner, backing up every move and telling them what they want to hear. There is little room for objectivity. While support from close associates is highly valued and very important, it is not enough to reinforce such a major decision. One disadvantage of not getting insight is a possible "repeat" in a future marriage.

Olivia, after having made the decision to divorce (with the help of a professional), told her family and close friend. Both had known in advance that some sort of decision was coming, but had successfully kept all opinions to themselves. When they were informed of the decision, the reaction was the same. It was subdued and still lacked even the words, "You are doing right." They were smart to restrain in this manner. While she was abashed at their lack of enthusiasm but rejoiced that a decision had been made, time and hindsight told her how correct they had been in their behavior. Divorce is a singular experience and has to be dealt with basically by the individual. Had Olivia been influenced by family and friends, she might have overlooked some very important factors that only she could deal with, with professional guidance.

SOMEBODY SAVE ME—Looking Elsewhere

An affair, or substituting the other partner with a new one, is not a good approach. This form of action truly prevents self-evaluation and growth by coping directly with the emotional problems of divorce. The basis for the new relationship is at best shaky. It is usually built on a common bond of unhappiness and problems from the bad marriages. While the new partners may find initial solace and comfort in sharing troubles with someone who has experienced the same anguishes, in the long run a solid foundation is lacking. There is usually a lack of self-knowledge and true understanding of the initial breakdown. In addition, feelings of guilt surround any divorce. If an affair is the means to an end, additional guilt will arise, creating even lower self-esteem. An elated feeling brought about by attracting and being attracted by another will at first exist, often overshadowing guilt, but it is there to emerge later in subtle, destructive ways.

If a new marriage takes place shortly after a divorce, a person is robbed of the process, painful though it may be, of learning to deal with life and oneself. If there is no immediate marriage, the affair usually runs its course, with both involved finding that eventually they have to deal with things they have previously set aside. The greatest tragedy here is that the opportunity to work through one's problems and feelings with the original partner has been lost. The possibility of salvaging the marriage is bypassed if one has focused energy and time on an affair.

When a person is considering divorce, the best attitude to develop is "I may want to remarry someday, but I certainly shouldn't plan on it." One woman said she'd rather be happy in a divorce than miserable in a marriage, or happily married rather than happily divorced. She was prepared for remaining single and not *counting* on remarriage.

I NEED HELP—Professional

The role of the professional counselor is to help a person make a realistic, responsible decision. Making the decision is hard. It is harder than almost any other decision a person has made in a lifetime. The first step is to *understand* as completely as possible what factors on each person's part contributed to the breakdown. The old adage "It takes two to cause a divorce" is certainly true. Objectivity can come only with guidance. This involves time with a counselor and even more time on "homework." We found that writing down feelings and events both past and present is helpful.

YOO-HOO, WHERE ARE YOU?

Once a person is actively working toward a decision, he or she becomes absorbed and almost obsessed. There is a constant mental battle. Reading books may become impossible; television is a thing of the past. Long walks for thinking may become important. We come up with the same thoughts over and over again and often doubt our mental stability. Every waking hour is spent rehashing the marriage—its good and bad points. Mental fatigue can become serious. You may wonder if you are a candidate for a mental hospital for even thinking some of your deepest thoughts. You may become extremely short-tempered and impatient. Your anger may be manifested in areas where you were once usually calm and in control. Fran's driving habits completely changed and she became enraged at other drivers on the road. Some people actually have accidents while so distracted. A crowded grocery store and even a few people ahead in line can become too much to cope with. The slightest problem with the children can be an aggravation which throws you completely out of control. There is the need for lashing out at others, and when this happens for a long time, you question whether a divorce will help to cure this type of action, or whether the behavior is the real "you." You wonder whether the unhappy marriage and the painful process of decision-making has affected you to the extent that this irritable reaction might be a permanent characteristic. The one who is lashing out can become guilt-ridden, especially if the other spouse has the temperament to accept these unpleasant responses and the patience to endure without retaliation or any positive suggestion for a solution. You doubt your own worth, lose self-confidence, and wonder if there is any solution, either in or out of the marriage. You may become so distracted at work that you can hardly get through the day. The problem becomes an obsession. A secretary may be able to type detailed information all day, not making errors, yet her mind never wavers from thoughts of possible divorce, and she is barely able to recall the subject matter of her day's work. Some turn to excessive drinking. These feelings not only may occur during the decision-making process but may start in the serious warning signals stage and continue for some time after a decision is reached.

People can be physically affected in a number of ways. There may be a drastic weight change, losing or gaining. Sexual desire is bound to be affected, possibly to the point of total abstinence or the reverse, in desperation. Complexions break out, and intestines growl. Many people develop the three o'clock syndrome. They wake up at 3 A.M. daily and stay awake for hours—thinking. Some people lose interest in their appearance. If there is little regard for the partner, not much attempt is made to please.

Children may suffer when the parents do not care for themselves individually or for each other. Feeding and caring for small children is a monumental chore, particularly for the mother. Older children's demands or problems, requiring mental agility, may be shoved off by an attitude of "I can't cope with that," or with a snarl.

At this point, when one partner is involved in self-analysis things can become more strained than ever before. How difficult it is to be living with the possibility that one partner may reach the decision to divorce independently of the other. To be living with a person who is totally self-absorbed can be devastating. However, to be self-absorbed does not necessarily mean that self-analysis is taking place. One woman was frequently called at work by her husband, who wanted to know if *she* had made any decisions or changed *her* mind. He was absorbed, but not in self-analysis.

Often when a marriage has reached the stage when divorce is a major and almost constant consideration, one partner plays an active role in the decision-making process; the other, passive. (There are occasions when both partners reach the decision together to divorce, but this is uncommon.) The active partner can become labeled the "malcontent" either by self or the other. Guilt runs rampant, clouding vision and feelings, slowing down the process.

I'VE GOT TO GET AWAY

Often, when a person is in the midst of intense analysis, physical distance from the other is needed to gain perspective. Some will take a trip alone or with the children; others will choose separation.

One successful method in the indecisive stage is a temporary separation. In effect, the couple live for an agreed period of time "as if" they were divorced. The only exception is that they might meet regularly with a trained counselor. Their visits, sometimes together and sometimes separate, enable them to "monitor" their reactions and experiences in this "experimental procedure." The crucial factor is that both partners *really* view this as a decision-making process and not as an opportunity to gather evidence for a decision already made. Otherwise, there is no value in the separation other than a temporary lull before the next storm.

TOO MUCH TOO LATE

The passive partner will often crowd the other with too much attention. Flowers might be sent; gourmet dinners cooked. One person couldn't even find time alone in the bathroom. One went on a trip only to find the partner joining her. Pressure like this from the passive partner seems only to reinforce the other's need for distance and therefore may hasten the decision for permanent separation.

Sometimes the passive person will switch to the active role by demanding a decision. "I have to know now. What have you decided?"

When the beginning of an understanding of what is wrong is achieved, the partners or the individuals again have one of three choices:

1. To commit to the relationship as it is
2. To try to change the relationship and themselves
3. To get a divorce

During the decision-making process a person will consider each of these, eventually eliminating until one choice remains.

I'M GONNA DO IT—LOVE ME OR LEAVE ME

Commitment to the relationship takes complete and total acceptance (not to be confused with resignation): "This is the way it is"; "This is the way it will be"; "I accept this"; "I can live with this and with my partner, requiring no change from either of us." This decision is unusual by the time the relationship has reached the serious warning signals stage. However, it is possible. The reasons may vary. Not wishing to hurt children by divorce may motivate one person. Inability to accept divorce may be another reason. A father not wanting to be separated from his children may be a third. Religious convictions may be influential.

WHETHER TO CHANGE OR TO DIVORCE

An attempt to change the relationship is an extremely difficult process. If achieved, the rewards should be golden. However, it takes a deep commitment from *both* partners, as well as a great deal of caring, self-knowledge, capability, and maturity. Even when the partners are armed with these, the process takes a long time. The partners have to be able and willing to forgive past differences and hurts and change their methods of communication and possibly some major habits.

If the decision to change the relationship is made, each partner must still have positive feelings for the other as well as the relationship. Professional counsel should be essential.

HOW DO I KNOW FOR SURE? . . . I DON'T

When people are choosing a course of action, not only should they delve into the structure, mechanics, and emotions as previously mentioned, but they should also consider all the ramifications of what they anticipate divorce to be like. "Will I be jumping from the frying pan into the fire?" Herein lies the seemingly impenetrable wall. You can't see through it, over it, or around it. Often you may feel that remaining in an unhappy marriage is easier and safer than facing the many "unknowns" of divorce. The only way is to proceed. But first, the pitfalls and problems of divorce need to be considered. This often is overwhelming and is at first impossible for a person to surmount. The fear of the all too familiar past, as well as of the unknown future, can put you back into the ambivalent state of indecision. Also, once the choice has been made to divorce, most persons continue to return to the other alternatives over and over again.

I'M NOT SURE I CAN HANDLE THIS

There are many reasons for delaying a decision.
Loneliness. Fear of loneliness is one concern that emerges.

"What will I do at night and on weekends?" "Whom will I talk to and confide in?" "Can I exist without the opposite sex?" The feeling may be that it is easier to leave things the way they are, for loneliness would be too much to bear.

Outside Opinion. A person may ask, "What will my friends think?" There may be fear of losing friends or embarrassment that divorce publicly admits a mistake. Another horrifying thought is that you might become the source of local gossip.

Parents. Parents and their feelings are often considered. "How will they react?" "Will they understand?" "Will they stand by me?" "Will they be angry?" "Will they be hurt?" The role for the parents of a divorcing person is not easy. They will feel their own anguish as a result of your unhappy state. A divorce will alter their position and relationship with you. They may wonder, "What can I do to help?" "How am I needed?" "Have I done anything wrong?" They may react with anger, or they may become overly concerned and smothering. They too may spend some sleepless nights.

Religion. There is a keen sense of guilt and personal embarrassment in regard to the wedding vows. Most of us have been taught the sanctity of marriage and are greatly influenced by the promises we made—"for better, for worse." One person said, "I didn't know worse could be this bad."

Time. There is never a convenient time to get a divorce. How difficult it is to suggest divorce when a child's birthday is coming up, or when Hanukkah or Christmas is just around the corner. The year is filled with momentous occasions—Easter, Mother's Day, Father's Day, summer vacation, Thanksgiving, etc. The thought of going through these events in turmoil is a great deterrent.

While time is passing by, an endurance test is also taking place. We term it endurance because it relates to the length and the quality of the marriage. It may be that the longer the partners are married, the easier it becomes to live with the situation, but not usually. In most cases, the longer the couple are married, under such strained circumstances the harder it is to cope. Either way, the endurance test goes on.

Children. When children are involved, the problems become

compounded. You will ask what effect a divorce will have on them. Will they be damaged if there is a divorce, or possibly more if there isn't one? Will they be able to accept it? You will feel it is cruel to separate them from one parent and the parent from them. Will the parent who receives custody be able to handle their growth effectively? Will the parent who is away remain interested in them, or be able to adjust without them? Will they hate the parent who breaks up their home? What if an older child chooses to live with the parent who does not have custody of the other children?

Events. Circumstances such as a major job change or a pregnancy may keep a person from making the decision. In particular, a husband making a job change can alter the family situation significantly. The new position may not be available if the employer views a divorced status as undesirable. Pressure by the husband might be made on the wife not to divorce, so as not "to ruin" his career. A husband might be unemployed. How could anybody "kick him while he is down"?

The pregnancy of the wife may keep the couple from divorcing. "How can we separate now?" "How could he leave me at a time like this?" The wife would probably have to lay aside plans to work immediately after the baby came. The financial picture becomes altered—both the future and the immediate. Suddenly there is a totally new dimension to the problem.

Crisis. Some people need a crisis to lean on to keep from making a decision. A crisis can be manufactured at every turn if one partner does not want a decision to be made or wants the other to feel guilty about even discussing divorce. If a child is having difficulty in school or has trouble relating to others, this can be blown out of proportion and become a "crisis" on which one partner can lean for support. The health of one of the partners or a family member may thwart a decision. If someone is battling an illness or a disease, the couple may put off getting a divorce. One couple did just this because one partner's father had recently had a heart attack. It may even be more convenient to get a divorce after a family member dies of a terminal illness. Other couples may delay because there has been a recent death.

Economics. The economics of getting a divorce may reach out to both partners in different ways. A couple feel they cannot "afford" to get divorced. Child support payments and maintenance for the wife may be more than the husband feels he can afford, especially while having to maintain a place of his own. A wife may feel insecure about being "on her own" and having to get a job, particularly if she has never worked or not worked in many years. If she has not been trained for the job market and fears she is unable to earn a sufficient income, she may feel a desperate sense of inadequacy or dependency. Both partners may not wish to alter their standard of living by having to set up separate households. There may be the loss of club memberships, and with the division of property and possessions, each will have less than they had together. The husband may feel great resentment at having worked many years to acquire things for his family and now be forced to consider giving them up. The wife may resent having worked early in the marriage, possibly "putting her husband through school," and then having to sacrifice by getting a divorce.

Good Qualities of the Other. Although the marriage reaches a low point and a lot of hostile feelings exist, most persons will recognize that there are good qualities in the other. How do they dare give these up? One person appreciated that her partner was willing to stay married even when the chips were down. That is not easily ignored. Physical qualities of the other may still appeal, or the person's mental capacity, humor or wit, thoughtfulness and consideration.

Concern Over the Other. If one spouse leans more toward divorce than the other does, that one may wonder what he or she will be "doing" to the spouse. There may be strong feelings of responsibility. One partner may threaten suicide, trying to thwart a decision to divorce. How can the partner know if the other really means it? Another may threaten suicide if there is no divorce.

The Mechanics of Living Alone. One may be concerned over the problems of coping with the checkbook, income tax, insurance, house, and car. Another may not wish to become cook, housekeeper, and launderer.

Lack of Self-Worth. The one partner may be so completely disgusted with himself that he may question whether a divorce would improve his temperament. His self-esteem may be so low that he cannot make such a "self-centered" decision to divorce when the life of the other would be affected.

Giving Up Too Soon. There is a concern that if you divorce, the other partner might "change," be "happy," or "do well" without you—or perhaps will change next month, if you "hang in there." If you divorce and the former spouse does change, it might mean that you were the problem all along. What a blow to face—after the fact. There are many pressures which make us feel that we should "put in more time," yet it might be time for time's sake only.

Appeal. Many persons may have lost confidence in their attractiveness or appeal. Will the opposite sex be interested in them? Will they have dates? What type of person will appeal to them?

Social Life. Women in particular are concerned that they will be "dropped" by their married friends, having to sit at home weekend after weekend. Will they be "forced" to go to singles bars to meet people? Will their standards be compromised in order to have a social life?

Divorce. Finally, who wants to be divorced? It's a stigma, an embarrassment, and an admission of failure, or so we think. The feeling that your life has become a cheap soap opera can develop. Who wants the world to see that?

Unfortunately, after rehashing all the concerns over a divorce, we find that there are almost *no answers* in advance. Solutions and answers can be anticipated and a few concrete efforts made, such as the wife's getting a job in advance or the husband's finding an apartment, but essentially the major concerns remain. One counselor told his patient: "You want everything tied into neat little packages. Life isn't like that." The decision has to be made on this basis, for there is absolutely no way to tell exactly "how things will be" if the decision to divorce is made.

THAT'S ALL THERE IS

After careful analysis of the relationship, self, and future possibilities, a person is then faced with the decision: "Should I get a divorce or not?" Usually the choice to divorce is made because the alternatives seem impossible to work out or accept. Divorce is the last resort. One person chose this action when it was realized that every alternative and every concern had been considered. There was nothing left to think about. Another became convinced, after her husband had started legal proceedings. The judge told her that "relationships don't usually change—for a few months, maybe, but not permanently." She could look back and recognize this pattern —"Here we go again." One person asked her counselor how much time she was supposed to give her marriage. He replied, "Do you think you've given it sufficient time?" She decided eight years of unhappiness was enough.

Often a counselor will force a decision by telling the person that another appointment does not have to be made until a decision is reached.

IF I CHOOSE NOT TO CHANGE, I MUST FEEL O.K.

After you have wrestled with the many factors involved in decision-making, you may decide not to get a divorce. At this point, acceptance needs to occur. "I know some of what I did wrong." "I know why this isn't working." "I understand I can't predict the future." "I understand I will be a divorced person." "I will be living alone."

A person should begin to feel better about self through the reinforcement of commitment to improving the situation through a decision. You have recognized and acknowledged your own value by no longer allowing destructiveness to be a part of your life. If the decision is divorce, you are choosing not to change yourself but to change your environment. This takes self-confidence. While the confidence will be new and shaky, it is there and is a good springboard to a new life. At best, divorce is a risk, a gamble, but should be a calculated one, carefully thought through. Once the decision is made, you should dedicate yourself to reinforcing your newfound confidence by your actions and life in the future.

THE ODD ONE OUT

There is one additional factor that needs to be touched upon. We have leaned toward the possibility of one person deciding to divorce rather than it being a mutual decision. What happens to the other partner? Surprisingly, the feelings and concerns are similar. Both will need to go through evaluation of the marriage. Both will need to make the decision to accept divorce and re-create self-esteem through self-knowledge and positive actions. Both will act after the decision to divorce or even after the legal process has started. *When* is unimportant; the process is the same.

CHAPTER 7

Limbo

Once you have made the decision to divorce, you are then left with the task of making your decision become action. At first you may feel happy, elated, and relieved that you have been able to resolve your dilemma after such long unhappiness. The euphoric feeling will probably last only a short time and then be replaced by anxieties over your decision. You still have to go through some very unpleasant actions. We call this time "limbo." It can last a few months or over a year, depending on how long it takes to get divorced. However, it can still be a constructive period where you begin your growth.

"Limbo" consists of:

1. Telling your spouse
2. Telling your children
3. Telling your family and friends
4. Legal action
5. Your public

I CAN'T TAKE IT ANYMORE—Telling Your Spouse

It is horrible for couples to tell their partners that they don't love them or can't stand to live with them. True, this has probably been said in subtle ways or even overt ways during the breakdown of the marriage, but the actuality of saying "I'm divorcing you" is a bitterly painful experience for both. Some spouses may avoid the confrontation completely by having a third party take the step for them. A lawyer might write a letter to this effect. Other spouses may write a letter themselves even if both still live in the same house. Some may just move out while the other is away. Those who do choose to deliver the ultimatum (and it does seem that) face-to-face may avoid the moment until an incident forces their decision. The partner may be planning an event or a party, and the reply of the other when approached could be, "Don't count on me. I won't be here." Or, "Don't program me into the future." Anger over an incident may provide the means for making an announcement. "I hate what you just did. I want a divorce." A partner may request the decision, "You are considering a divorce. What have you decided?" Whatever the means a person chooses, it is very uncomfortable, and the time is never really right.

WE CAN'T LIVE TOGETHER ANYMORE—
Telling Your Children

Telling your children that you are divorcing is another tremendous commitment to the decision. It is confusing and painful to the children even if they are acutely aware that problems exist between their parents. If it is at all possible, for the protection of the children, it is best that they not become involved in the vacillation of their parents before a firm decision is made and stuck to. Once the children are told and they know it's a concrete fact, their adjustment will be helped. They may or may not be able to realize that no matter how much they wish or believe that their parents will reunite, it will not be.

It is advantageous if both parents can agree on how to tell the children of their divorce and then do it together. Emotions will be high and probably tears will flow. It may help the children to know that the parents feel terrible too. Young children usually can't grasp the meaning of divorce and might laugh out of confusion or even be totally uninterested. Don't become upset or offended. Just be alert to their questions in the future, and let them learn through experience. Children, no matter what their age, will not be able at first to grasp completely the ramifications of divorce. One small boy turned to his mother and said with delight, "Now we will be able to get a raccoon!"

While you are going through your adjustment, your children will have adjustments as well as worries and problems of their own. An excellent book is available for children called *The Boys and Girls Book About Divorce,* by Dr. Richard Gardner. You might be amazed at the concerns children will have. This book is written on a child's level and is well worth having on the bookshelf. Some children may wish to read it on their own; others may wish to share it with their parents. If there is a large age span, the older children may benefit by reading it to their younger siblings. Also, it would be beneficial for each parent to have a copy so the children will have an opportunity to work through their concerns with each of them.

SURPRISE . . . WE ARE GETTING A DIVORCE—
Telling Your Family and Friends

After the immediate family have gone through their shock, the rest of the family are next on the list to be told. Get to them quickly before your children tell all the neighbors and friends.

Family reactions can be varied. Some may feel that your divorce is their failure as well as yours. What did they do wrong when rearing you? Why can't you get along with your wonderful husband or wife? Other families may feel guilty: "Why didn't we see this and do something to prevent it?" Some families for a variety of reasons may be vastly opposed to your divorce, while others may be sympathetic and supportive. The kindest way to handle your family is not to get them too involved in all the problems of the past marriage as well as in the divorce proceedings. You do need support, but save all the "dirty" stuff for a counselor. If your family take the stand that it's all your fault, this will be hard, but try not to justify everything to them. It probably won't work. If given time, they may come around and not be as critical as they once were. There are also the families who will try to move in and solve all your problems for you. This won't help you in the long run. You have to start solving your own problems and this is a good place to begin. You can be kind, but firm.

Friends are put in a terrible spot over divorce. Usually they try not to "take sides." In some cases this works; in others it creates resentment from the divorcing partners. Eventually you will find that there are friends who will take sides. They will probably be the persons who are much closer to one of you. Actually, we feel this is good. Each of you will need friends who are interested in your welfare. They may not dislike the other but recognize their commitment to the person they are closer to. Peripheral friends may be able to remain removed and supportive to both. These you also need to keep your world from getting too narrow. It is often difficult to remain objective about the friends who "straddle the fence." In time, though, you will be able to see the value in this type of friendship. We will go into more detail in Chapter 10, under "Dealing with Friends, Social Life, and Relatives," about how to include your friends in your divorced life.

I THINK I NEED A LAWYER—Legal Action

Why might you need a lawyer?
Before the divorce:

1. To work out temporary maintenance
2. To work out a property settlement
3. To work out custody of the children
4. To work out visitation rights
5. To protect you from a partner who becomes physically abusive
6. To help settle a dispute over who moves out

After separation:

1. To enforce the divorce agreement of judgment if it is not being adhered to
2. To review visitation rights if one parent is abusing the agreement
3. To negotiate on one parent's actions involving the children
4. To help collect maintenance if it is not being paid

5. To obtain increased maintenance and/or child support or to cut it down
6. To protect one partner if the other is physically abusive

While in the decision-making stage, you may or may not have talked to a lawyer about the legal process. Each state varies in its laws, so it is impossible for us to outline an absolute process. It is important to find a lawyer who is competent at divorce and who is compatible with you. Since there is no "clearinghouse" for lawyers and their credentials, ask other divorced friends who their lawyers were and how they liked them. Then shop around. When you meet with a lawyer for the first time or two, an important test is to ask for an outline of what the legal procedure will be, i.e., what you should expect from beginning to end. You are not obligated to move on unless you are ready. One word of caution. The process of the law is not absolute but depends on the actions from "the other party" and that person's lawyer. So you must be prepared to adjust and make allowances. Be certain that your lawyer is patient and interested enough in your case to take the time to explain in advance all the different sets of circumstances that can arise. Examples can be: If both parties agree on divorce and property settlement, it will take so many months. If the property settlement is not reached by such and such a time, we will go to court for a pre-trial, then later for a trial.

Don't panic if events don't happen exactly as your lawyer outlined them in advance. Be certain the lawyer will keep you advised and informed. Ask questions. Push for explanations. If answers don't seem to come openly, you may want to look elsewhere. Discuss the fees for services and who should pay them.

It has been said that the only friendly divorces occur when there is no problem over the property. This is usually the case only when the marriage has been very short and there are no children, or if both partners are independently able to provide for themselves and do not feel a strain on their finances. The majority of the cases go the other way. There is likely to be a great deal of antagonism and unpleasantness. Men may feel the need to guard their future by not giving any more than they can afford. Women usually feel insecure and vulnerable. Just plain bitterness can be acted out through the settlement. This is one of the many places where a separated couple can hurt each other. Often women are amazed that their husbands, after providing for them throughout the marriage, are no longer willing to ante up. It comes as quite a shock and emotional trauma. It can easily leave you feeling at sea and completely vulnerable as well as hurt. If a woman remains financially dependent on her ex-husband for years after the divorce, she may continue to feel vulnerable. He may feel a growing resentment at the demands she continues to make. Both may want the results of the settlement to go their way so that their standard of living is not reduced. Each might find that instead of being reasonable they fight for their individual concerns, thus prolonging their agony.

After a period of bickering one might feel: "Oh, just forget it. Things aren't as important as the pain all this fighting is giving me." The tendency at this time might be to give in too much and settle for less than is reasonable. Don't succumb to this urge if you feel it. You will have many years to regret it.

YOUR PUBLIC

Through the entire time of public adjustment, expect to be uncomfortable. You will feel that DIVORCE is stamped on your forehead in neon letters. For several years it may even be difficult for you to be able to say, "I am divorced." You will feel that people are talking about you. You'll be right. Some are. Have hope; somebody else will be getting a divorce next month and will steal all the attention!

One way to handle the insecurity you feel is to reply to questions such as "Who is your spouse?" or "What does your husband do?" by simply saying, "I'm not married." Let them figure out where the children in the backseat of the car came from. Even several years after your divorce, people you don't see often will ask, "How is Elaine?" You will probably still find it embarrassing or even painful to catch them up on the past few years of your life.

Right after your separation, party invitations will present a problem. It's a shocker to a hostess when you respond to an invitation with "Thank you so much, what a great invitation. I would love to accept, but there is a problem. Harry and I are getting a divorce." If she is a lady of the world, she will grab her kitchen sink and reply, "We would still love to have you both." At that point, you may want to say, "Wonderful, I'll accept for myself and give the message to Harry and have him call you." Or you could ask her to call Harry at his office and invite him. Since you are separated, now is the time to start your life on these new terms. You have to do it sometime. By going separately to social events, you will spread the news of your situation more quickly and educate your public much sooner. While this is embarrassing and painful, it won't last long.

In many cases feelings are so raw that the partners might not wish to be at the same gatherings. If this is your feeling, you might decide mutually who accepts what invitation, or quietly decline for yourself. Most people do not know how to handle the entertaining of separated couples without taking sides and may decide not to invite them at all. Some hostesses, however, inadvertently create painful situations for their friends by inviting both partners individually to the same function even after the separation has become public. If you find you can't enjoy yourself with the other present, just ask the hostess if she is inviting the other and then decline if she is. If you explain that you cannot handle this type of situation yet, she will probably understand. If she doesn't, forget it.

It may seem odd that we have given this much attention to invitations at a time when so many other things loom much larger in your life. We feel that any separated person's social life is important. You will need contact with others. You will need the feeling that they still care. You will need an area in your life that isn't disrupted by your divorce. Your social life can help fill these needs.

Beware of the "do-gooders," who for secret reasons of their own hate to see anybody get divorced. They may take it upon themselves to bring about a reconciliation. You can firmly say, "I'm flattered you are concerned, but it's so painful I can't discuss it." Or, if you are feeling particularly strong that day, you may wish to say something like, "Bug off."

Another type of person may surface. This is the person who is unhappy and wants advice or just someone to share with. The best thing is to suggest sympathetically that the person seek a counselor. Don't allow yourself to be dragged into someone else's problem when you're still trying to sort things out in your own mind.

There are some people who want all the details. "What happened?" "We all thought you were so happily married." Don't tell them anything. The cardinal rule of divorce is to say absolutely nothing critical or destructive. Statements such as, "It's very sad —too sad even to talk about" will dispose of them. Saying nothing may take all the strength you have left, especially if your ex-spouse is talking about you or has hurt you badly. Overcome the urge to retaliate. You will only damage yourself. You will eventually feel uncomfortable with yourself, and so will others. Hold your head high and carry on tight-lipped. Your actions will speak louder than words.

Part Two

AFTER DIVORCE

CHAPTER 8

Now That I'm Separated, How Will I Make It?

Your divorce is in the works. Now what? You need to deal with the many feelings and questions that go hand in hand with being separated. After self-evaluation, you should know and understand where you have been before you can decide in what direction you want your life to go.

Divorce is the archenemy of self-esteem. No matter who decided to get the divorce, both persons have to face the fact that they have failed at one of the most important undertakings in life. You will have intense feelings of unworthiness, uselessness, and failure, as well as insecurity about your future. It is vital to live your life conscientiously from now on to make you feel good about yourself. Others can try to rebuild your shattered ego, and this is important, but only you can be responsible for your rehabilitation and future growth. This cannot be done in a week or months. Having been divorced over four years, we have found that two years is about the minimum time for successful adjustment. You may feel overwhelmed and discouraged. Will you ever be able to work out all your problems and emotions? In time, yes. At first your progress will be erratic. You may make great strides in one area and none in another, to find later that things have reversed. You may feel you are totally in control one day, only to lose ground the next. In growth, it's normal to take three steps forward and two steps back.

There will be at least seven issues that you will have to deal with as a divorced person. Some of these issues you have already considered. Suggested solutions will be discussed throughout the rest of the book.

Your main goal should be to achieve understanding and a constructive life plan. This will come through experience and dealing successfully with the issues as they arise. We have categorized the main issues that a divorced person has to confront and work through, creating self-esteem through success. The longer you put off facing the tasks before you, the longer it will take.

1. Loneliness
2. A new home
3. Learning to live on a new income
4. Dealing with your children
5. Dealing with your ex-spouse
6. Dealing with friends, social life, relatives
7. Dating

The first question you'll ask yourself prior to facing the above tasks is, "When do I really become single?" We have found that some people feel single before the divorce is filed; others may not feel emotionally single until the last paper is signed and the lawyer calls to say the divorce is final; others may not feel single until months later. *When* you feel single depends on *how* you are going to cope with your entrance into a new life-style. No one takes care of you but yourself. You may feel somewhat lost, sad, frightened, lonely, and bored. Your feelings can be in a state of inner conflict. You might want to be around other adults and at the same time don't want to be around anyone. The house is clean, or maybe it isn't; the quiet is driving you up the wall; the children are getting on your nerves; your family and friends don't seem to show as much attention anymore; you feel alone and abandoned; it may be hard to manage your finances; you can't read another book or watch another television show; sometimes you cry a lot; you have thought and thought through everything in the past until you are weary and blue in the face. All those things you wondered about having to cope with while you were in the process of deciding to get a divorce really are here to haunt you. You may find that you have trouble concentrating on your work. You feel ineffective and useless.

You may wonder not so much *how* you will make it as you do

if you will make it. You can make it if you really want to. Now is the time to set some goals for yourself. Set priorities. Be realistic. Nothing happens overnight. Realize that sometimes you will be discouraged. It will take time and "working at it" for things to change; but don't ever forget that your situation *can* change if you want it to. You are the only person who can get you up in the morning and started on the way to a constructive day. No person can *make* another happy. It's up to you. As the saying goes, "Today is the first day of the rest of your life," so don't blow it! Taking the initiative is not easy; but go ahead and give it a try.

LONELINESS

During the process of setting up life alone and for a long time thereafter you will find that you are lonely. Loneliness often appears as soon as the initial euphoric feeling has disappeared. You may have even experienced it in the marriage. It will now be a constant companion, but slowly you will learn to cope with loneliness.

Do you feel lonely in situations like these? When . . .

Your friends don't seem to care.
Your family doesn't seem to care.
You have no one to share the moment with.
You have no one to give you support.
You don't think you can cope.
Your dates don't respond as you had hoped.
You don't have dates.
You don't have a close, intimate relationship.
You go to bed alone.
You wake up alone.
Your children are being difficult.
You are alone over a weekend or on a holiday.
You haven't heard from your children for a long time.
You are out with friends, and everybody has a partner except you.
You are with single friends, and their lives seem meaningless.

Loneliness is one of the major demons for divorced people. It is a feeling to fear and hate. It's scary and depressing. It's inevitable. If loneliness is not met head on with determination, it can bring a person down to the point of not functioning, not wishing to live and just giving up. Loneliness will hit both the person living with children and the person alone.

Building up your self-esteem will be one way to combat loneliness, because you will be concentrating on things other than yourself. The mottoes "Keep busy" and "Plan ahead" are good ones. A word of caution. Be careful to fill your time with activities that really interest you. Avoid spinning your wheels by rushing from one event to another without much thought. Often there is a particular time of the day or of the week when you are more susceptible than other times. Once you realize when that time is, beat the demon by planning an activity that will keep you moving. If your susceptible time is when you come home to an empty place after work, plan something to get involved in the minute you walk in the door. Cook a pleasing meal for yourself or your family. Garden, clean, do the laundry, go to a movie, read a book, go swimming, exercise—but plan ahead. If your vulnerable time is early morning, plan the night before what you are going to do the minute you wake up, and do it.

Do you know why you feel lonely and alone? As painful as it is to admit it to yourself, you may realize that you were dependent on your spouse for many things. Even in marriages with many problems there were two people. Now you have to make all the decisions. You want to do what is best for you, and your children. You may have a feeling of abandonment and not be able to see any options for relief. Sometimes you wonder if the world is real.

Mary Jane could not stand being by herself another minute. She began to date anyone who would ask her out, and when no one called she went to one of the singles bars, where she found others who felt lonely and alone. However, she soon became unhappy with herself. In the beginning she felt relief from loneliness and thoroughly enjoyed her new freedom. Gradually, she discovered that many of the "friends" she made had as many problems as she. One day she decided to make a list of what she was doing and what she would like to do. She decided that she would like to meet some new people and found that many options were open to her. Maybe she would go back to school, or at least enroll in some "fun" classes. There were a lot of things that she had always secretly wanted to try. By watching the newspaper she found that many free events were available. She decided to plan each day and little by little filled her days with constructive things to keep her busy. She took better care of herself. Sometimes she still felt lonely, but the feeling no longer got the best of her. She found that if she gave herself something to look forward to, she could usually get the best of the feeling.

There are other options open to those who choose. A paid or a volunteer job for males and females can serve as an outlet for time and energy. Sometimes having to meet a schedule is the best thing that can happen. You may not feel like getting up in the morning, but you have made a commitment, and once you are at work your day will go better. A job also offers contact with other adults without the element of emotional involvement. A job or a job change just may be your salvation during this difficult period of adjustment. Even women who have never worked or have to leave small children at home with a baby-sitter or at a day care center often find that they are better mothers when they have contact with other adults at least part of the day. Patsy was already working at the time of her divorce but was in a one-girl office with two men. She had no one to go to lunch with and often ate at her desk in order to avoid eating alone in a restaurant. She did not brood over her present situation but took action to bring about a positive result. Her smartest move was to find a job with considerably more employees. Just their companionship at work was a boost to her.

Working men might find that a volunteer job on weekends gives them meaning and contact with new people. Pursuing a new hobby or an athletic interest can be rewarding.

You're not dating and may not even be the least bit interested. Do you sit at home and wait for something to happen? Your old friends may feel uncomfortable about including you. Don't wait for them. Make the first move. Entertaining can be fun and give you something to look forward to as well as reinforce self-confidence.

Even with much consideration and effort invested in overcoming loneliness, there will be times when it will take hold of you. Sometimes you may want to allow it to wash over you without resisting. But don't let loneliness buffet you too long.

CHAPTER 9

A New Home and a Different Income

Usually one person remains in the present home. Yet there are two new homes to be established. The partner who does not have to change the physical environment has a great deal of work ahead to create new emotional surroundings.

WHERE WILL I LIVE?

For the partner who has to "move out" the initial adjustment is often the most difficult. You not only have to relocate, leaving most of the familiar, tangible things of life, but also you are usually the partner who lives without the children. It is often a good idea to find a temporary place to live until some thought can be given to the requirements of a new home. Some people stay with the spouse until there has been time to think through what is wanted. Furnished and unfurnished apartments are available as well as hotels or the homes of single friends or family. Whatever temporary abode is chosen, this should be kept for a relatively short period of time. The permanent choice of where to live is the first tangible step toward adjustment and should be a serious concern. A lack of permanence and belonging can soon become depressing and a hindrance rather than the help it started out to be.

Most people usually choose to live alone. However, there are those who live with family or a single friend. Too often living with family, particularly parents, is not satisfactory. Most parents just don't seem to be able to stop parenting even if you are thirty-five and have three children. Living with family can be a good interim arrangement while you need the support of others, but on a long-term basis it is not very workable, unless absolutely necessary.

When you are considering where to live, the first thing to decide is the life-style you want along with your budget.

1. Do I want to be a swinging single?
2. Do I want to establish a home where my children will be safe and comfortable?
3. Do I want to be near my place of work?
4. Do I need a touch of the outdoors or of city life?
5. Do I want a built-in opportunity for group companionship?
6. Do I want to be left alone by my neighbors?
7. Do I want to live alone?

There are many condominiums, apartments, and neighborhoods that offer each of the above. Deciding can be a major undertaking. Asking other single friends about their homes can often be of help.

Usually at this stage the divorce is in process, or will be soon. You may not be sure what your financial situation will be. This can be a great excuse to avoid making the first tangible step toward single life. It is possible to estimate how the money can be divided. If you have to make a change after the settlement, O.K. Not as much will be lost compared to what you have gained through setting up life for yourself. Also, if you make a mistake, you can always undo it.

Once you have chosen a new home, try to think of it as just that, and concentrate on living alone rewardingly.

You will be establishing a pattern that will eventually become familiar and comfortable. For men, there is the confusion of having to do things that have always been "women's work"—the laundry, shopping, equipping the kitchen and the household. Even the selection of cleaning supplies can be overwhelming. There will be linens and furniture to bring from your previous home or to buy. For many, these decisions can cause so much frustration and despair that one does not know where to start or which way to turn. Don't be afraid to ask for help. The advice of a female friend, one's mother, or a male friend who has gone through the same "ordeal" can be most beneficial. Take your time on these decisions, but continually work in the direction of completing your household. We have listed some basic items that might help you on your way.

Kitchen
Food shelves
  your choice of canned goods
  flour (plain, not self-rising)
  1 box salt
  black pepper
  catsup
  mustard and mayonnaise
  sugar (white granulated)
  coffee (ground or instant)

Refrigerator and freezer
  cheese
  eggs (one dozen; they keep well)
  margarine
  milk (optional)
  bread (this freezes well)
  potatoes (large Idahos for baking; smaller, round ones for frying or boiling)
  frozen or canned juice
  choice of meats and poultry (or TV dinners)

Equipment
  measuring spoons (one set)
  2 medium-sized pans
  1 skillet
  1 cookie sheet (for heating rolls)
  coffeepot (if you like the real thing)
  spatula
  toaster
  long-handled cooking fork
  3 large spoons for stirring and serving
  3 knives, from small to chopping size
  canisters for flour, sugar, etc.
  salt and pepper shakers
  creamer and sugar bowl
  4 to 8 knives, forks, and spoons

4 to 8 dinner plates
4 to 8 salad plates
4 to 8 cups and saucers
1 dozen glasses
can opener
bottle opener
paper towel holder and paper towels
paper napkins
4 to 8 table mats (you can use paper napkins unfolded or paper towels)
medium-sized pyrex dish (round)
dish rack and drainer, if you don't have a dishwasher

Cleaning Supplies
sponge and/or dishcloths
4 dish towels
liquid dishwashing soap
abrasive cleanser
window cleaner
liquid spray cleaner
sponge floor mop
broom
dustpan
vacuum cleaner

Bathroom
Equipment
toilet bowl cleaner and brush
toilet paper
sponge
abrasive cleaner
plumber's friend (don't wait until you need it; get it now!)
deodorizer

Linens
Don't forget the "White Sales" in January and August
3 bath towels
3 washcloths
3 terry cloth hand towels
bath mat for floor

rubber mat for tub
shower curtain and liner

Bedroom
Linens
   2 top sheets for each bed
   2 bottom sheets for each bed
   2 pillowcases for each pillow
   2 blankets
   1 mattress pad for each bed

Laundry
   low-suds detergent
   bleach (this should be used sparingly on whites)
   cling-free agent for use in dryer
   laundry basket or bag (if you use a laundromat)

You probably won't want to buy all these items the day you sign your lease, but you will eventually need them unless you plan to sleep on a bare mattress and eat TV dinners with your fingers. Your morale might suffer if you choose this course.

Look forward to the day when you refer to your new residence as "home." It will come if you expend some energy into making it just that. Think positively!

For those of you who are left at home with the children and house, you too will have a lot of adjusting to do. There may be many things you have never had to cope with before, such as general upkeep, furnace, car, and yard. Before you have problems, it would be wise to compile a list of repairmen for each type of appliance, the furnace, etc. You can get the names from your friends or departing partner. Your car is going to require regular maintenance. Find a reliable mechanic. For minor emergencies, such as a dead battery, flat tire, or being out of gas, cultivate a relationship with a neighborhood service station or have a membership in AAA. It is most reassuring that you know immediately where to get help if something goes wrong. If the yard seems to be too much, often you can find neighborhood children who want to earn money. It would be wise, however, to learn how to operate the lawn mower and when to have it serviced.

Your house may seem a burden at first, but if you plan ahead for maintenance and the breakdown of things, it will seem more manageable. You may find that you want or need to sell your house or change your apartment. Give yourself a little time before you make the final decision so you are certain you are making the right move for yourself and family.

How Can I Meet Expenses?

Almost all divorced persons have less income to live on than they did when they were married. Don't feel sorry for yourself. Find ways to make adjustments in your life-style and still get the most out of what you have to spend.

When Jane and Joe decided to end their marriage of eight years, they sold their house and moved into separate apartments. They divided what they had accumulated; both were faced with needing household items and furniture to replace what the other had taken. The cost of getting the divorce in addition to the cost of moving had set each back substantially. They were both working at the same jobs they had before the divorce. Each soon realized that living on a combined income was much different from living on their separate incomes. Each was now trying to meet the basic expenses of rent, gas and electricity, telephone, insurance, etc. Money didn't seem to be going very far, and each separately resented having to change life-style. They had been so involved in ending the marriage that they had never imagined that the financial adjustments would be serious. Complaining didn't seem to solve any problems. The temptation to try to get more income by taking Joe back to court came to Jane's mind often. On the other hand, Joe sometimes considered not sending Jane her monthly check. Each felt, Why should I have to make changes?

Your circumstances may be entirely different from Jane and Joe's. You may still be in your house with the children. You may have moved into a furnished apartment and left all behind. You will still need to take a good look at how you are spending your income and work at getting the most out of it. One way to face this problem is to make a list of your expenses. Then keep a record of every penny you spend over several months. Look at your list. Have you been shopping for bargains in food and clothing? Did you rush out and buy a new vacuum cleaner or toaster, or did you watch for ads in the paper and locate a reconditioned one? Is there anything on your list of expenditures that you now feel was an unnecessary purchase? Remember that fifty cents here and a dollar there can add up. Knowing what you have to spend and seeing where it goes can help you make any necessary adjustments. You may find that by saving small amounts you will soon have more money available for what you need or want. We are not saying that adjusting your life-style will be easy. We are saying that financial problems can become compounded if not faced from the beginning and necessary adjustments made.

Budgets are great as long as things go as you expect. All too often they don't. While you may find it impossible to save much on your income, it still would be wise to save a small amount to have on hand for emergencies. You will feel much better if you know that several hundred dollars are in the bank in case of illness or if the furnace blows up.

Credit is another important issue. Most men should not have any trouble if they have already established a good credit record, but what about the woman who has lived under her husband's wings? Suddenly you find that all the charge accounts have been closed. A lot of women will despair. We have found that if you apply immediately for credit, you won't have too much trouble. Start where you feel you will get the best response. Friends may offer advice as to where to start. Once you have several accounts opened, the others should follow suit. If you do run into difficulty, don't give up. It is against the law for companies to refuse credit to divorced women who do not have bad histories of nonpayment. Once you have established your credit, don't abuse it. If you find that you need or want something and don't have the money for it right now, the temptation will be to charge it. It would be advisable to do without until the money is in the bank. You can get in deep quickly. If you are on a tight budget, how will you ever get caught up? Consider this an opportunity to prove to yourself that you are capable of handling your own life responsibly. If children are involved, you most certainly must be prudent.

In the chapter on dealing with your ex-spouse, we stated that your relationship with each other continues through the existence of children and financial ties.

Money can prove to be a fertile battleground where anger and frustration and even hurt can be brought out against the other. Joe in the preceding vignette considered withholding payments to Jane. Some men may actually do this because of a lack of desire to cut their living standards. Others may withhold with the intention to punish. "She wanted the divorce. She can just cope with it. She and the children are no longer my responsibility." If this is carried to an extreme, consult your lawyer. Women often use finances in the same manner. Some subtly try to take advantage of their former husbands by encouraging the children to ask for things such as clothing or vacations. They can build up a father as the ogre of the year if he refuses. "He manages to do what he wants, but he won't give us enough to live on." "He doesn't care about you." If you have any of these feelings, take a good look at your true intent. Are you being fair? Have you tried to be honorable? It might not be a bad idea for divorced couples to discuss their finances together if they find there is a needed change. If you listen with an open mind, you might find that he is doing all that he can or that she really does need more help, for herself and the children.

CHAPTER 10

New Relationships

After your divorce, you will need to develop new relationships. Dealing with your children, with your ex-spouse, and with friends, social life, and relatives will all be major tasks for you to face.

DEALING WITH YOUR CHILDREN

We hate to call children an issue, but they are—a major one. One of the first things to be decided between the parents or by the court is who gets custody of the children. Naturally it is best if the parents can bury the hatchet temporarily and reach a mutual decision as to the living arrangement. There are many workable solutions. The obvious and most common is for the children to live with one parent and "visit" the other. Some parents trade their children back and forth for extended periods of time. One parent might keep the children one year, the other the next. One might keep the children during the winter and the other the summer. Others may prefer a weekend arrangement, the children spending the week with one parent and weekends with the other. It is natural for each parent to fear the loss of affection of the children to the other parent. The at-home parent has the "advantage" of being with the children daily. The away parent has the "advantage" of not being with them daily. Each is threatened by the other's position often and may try to shield the children from the other or bribe them. If the children are to live with the parents alternately, it is essential that they understand why. They may assume that the parents are trading them back and forth because neither really wants them, rather than that they both want them very much.

Since the most prevalent arrangement is that of the children living with one parent and visiting the other, we will deal directly with this.

Initially your children will be going through the adjustment of living with one parent rather than two. The age of the child or children and their parents' approach will greatly determine what effect the divorce has upon them.

Both parents have a huge adjustment to make in their lives with their children. They need your help, and you need theirs. The first rule to set for yourself is never to run down the other parent. The children come out the losers. The closed-mouth method can be hard, especially if the other parent is critical about you, wanting the children to know all the bad things you did and "continue" to do to them. If criticism is present, the children may become confused and resentful, often championing the parent who is under fire. The child who is the same sex as the criticized parent may feel that the criticism is directed toward him, too. When the opportunity arises, praise for genuine qualities in a parent should be offered to the children. Although the partners had their problems, there are usually some good attributes which can be honestly promoted. Some parents feel that they need support from their children concerning the decision to divorce or over issues that arise through subsequent years. They may tell the children all the "facts," expecting the children to support their position. How unfair! A child should be allowed to love both parents and not be asked to take sides and especially not be asked which parent he or she loves more. This shows a terrible insecurity on the parent's side, not to mention the trauma the child experiences for having to answer the question. If this rule isn't followed, it is likely that in later years all your criticism may "come to roost" by your children losing respect for you. Children have a way of growing up and seeing things more clearly.

Another temptation the parents can easily succumb to is feeling sorry for the children because of the divorce. Don't. It's too bad. It is hard on them, and they do need an alert ear and much understanding and love, but they will readily overcome it if you require it of them. The attitude "I know it hurts, and I'm sorry, but carry on, kid" is the best.

By all means don't pry into personal matters, particularly those of the other parent. It may be tempting to ask, "Whose car is in the driveway?" "What has your mother been doing?" Or, "Did your father ask about me?" Contain your curiosity. Children will eventually offer the information they want you to have.

The parent who has custody may sometimes feel torn in many directions. Do you come first, or do the children come first? Do you feel guilty when they get on your nerves to the point that you may be sorry you ever had them? Sometimes it seems that you never have a peaceful moment alone. They are always there. They sometimes seem demanding. Parents often have an intense feeling of "There isn't enough of me to go around." You worry if they aren't always happy. You feel so responsible. You hope they don't develop the bad traits of your ex-spouse. It is your fault if they misbehave or have trouble in school. You wish they would be "good." Remember that all children pass through certain stages of development. All children are happy and sad. So hang in there, and do the best you can.

You will find that you must learn to handle almost all situations alone. You must make singular decisions concerning small or important aspects of your children's lives. The lack of a sounding board is acutely felt. In some cases the away parent can continue to supply this need. If the parents find it impossible to communicate constructively, it is often helpful to rely on a family member or friend who knows the children. The person can at least listen to your concerns and help with perspective. For continuity's sake, choose a friend whose friendship is consistent in your own life.

Another aspect of living alone with children is the lack of a backup person. In other words, somebody who reinforces your decision or position on an issue, giving you more credibility or clout. Unfortunately, there is no substitute for this. You do have to go it alone. One psychologist said, "The father's most important role is to protect the mother from the children and the children from the mother." This buffer is gone no matter which parent has the children. The main things for you to aim toward are consistency and forcefulness in your stands. Your children will feel more secure.

A word here to the parent who does not live with the children. Occasionally you will become aware of a rule or a decision your partner has made with which you disagree. It is hard to be in the dark where your children are concerned and have no input or say-so. Be aware of the difficult role the other parent has and refrain from contradicting and undermining the other's authority. If you feel strongly, speak to the other parent about your concerns. If you are not heard, then you can decide either to drop it or consult your attorney. If you choose the latter, neither parent should involve the children in the discussions. The disagreement should be worked out as quietly as possible.

It is essential for divorced parents to learn to stand up for their own rights. When you have had enough, leave, go to the movies, or take a vacation without the children. They need time away from you just as much as you need time away from them. Parents often feel guilty concerning the divorce and try to "make it up to the kids." Do all you can to resist this temptation. It will ultimately hinder the adjustment and development of all involved.

Barbara has custody of her children. She made a hard-and-fast rule not to date on the weekends she had them. She felt guilty about having so little time during the week with her children, since she worked full time and wanted to "make it up" on the weekends they were with her. Inevitably she was asked for a date when it was her weekend with the children. She refused, until she realized that she was thwarting her own development and experiencing feelings of resentment toward the children. She concentrated on spending quality time during the day on Saturdays with them and treated herself to an evening out and a much-needed break.

Children are affected by divorce, but it need not be permanent. The role of divorced parents is to be as available as possible to the children and alert to their concerns, while not being dominated.

Lying down with a child as you put him to bed will offer a great opportunity to talk. You may find that the child is worried about losing the parent he lives with or losing the love of the away parent. He may be embarrassed that his parents are divorced or even feel responsible for the divorce. He may continue to hope that his parents will get back together. Whatever his concerns are, you should offer opportunities for them to be expressed. If you feel that problems are developing that you can't handle, seek a professional.

Children can recognize when a parent is struggling or down, and they can be thoughtless or even cruel. It's not unusual for a child who has been reprimanded to rush to his room crying, "I want my daddy." You may feel crushed, hurt, or even angry. The best response is either none at all or a quiet statement of "I know you do." Most likely the child is doing the same thing in reverse when with Daddy.

Another child may come home from a glorious weekend with her father and announce, "I want to go live with Daddy." Refrain from calling the child an ingrate or attacking the father. A proven successful response is, "I'm glad you had such a good time with him." You will need patience and a lot of fortitude.

During separation and divorce, adult emotions are usually near the surface. Additional demands made by children can be extremely difficult to handle. However, you can work on your self-esteem by feeling successful where your children are concerned. It often requires self-discipline not to "blow off" unjustly or to be overly unreasonable. One method of creating a mutually constructive life is literally to review each day at its end, emphasizing to yourself where you are satisfied with your decisions and behavior and where you are not. Be aware that you will never be able to create a perfectly tranquil life for yourself and your children (who can), but after a divorce many changes need to occur. Your life has been a turmoil of feelings, indecision, and disruptive behavior. It will now take a conscious effort on your part to calm down and redirect your living.

Eventually, if you "modify" your behavior, a constructive life pattern will become natural. We know two women who had snippy teen-age daughters. Both women found it very hard not to get constantly involved in verbal battles with their daughters. Finally, they made a chart at work. Each woman would award herself a gold star for the previous day if she had been able to hold her tongue. If she had lost her gold star, she would share with the other the frustration that got her. The daughters never knew about it, but life at home became much less of a battlefield.

What we are saying is that while some adjustment comes with time, a conscious effort has to be made to help it along.

While the role of the away parent is somewhat similar, in that communication is essential, the situation is also very different. An entirely new life-style has to be established. One of the main elements to consider is the ages of the children. With young children, their schedule is controlled by the other parent. To work out visiting arrangements takes cooperation. With older and teen-age children, get-togethers can be worked out between parent and child. Because of the demands of teen-age life, this is a lot more difficult and requires a great deal more understanding and flexibility from you. Consistency toward children of all ages by the away parent is the backbone of the long-term relationship. Keep your promises; keep in touch on a regular basis; and be consistent.

For the younger child, "visitation rights" (a horrible term to use concerning parent and child) should be worked out to suit both parents. We have found that if both parents are reasonable and cooperative, it is best not to have specific "rights." Every Saturday afternoon, for example, can become a binding drudgery to all concerned. Holidays might be the exception here so the children don't have to consume two turkey dinners each Thanksgiving or Christmas. Some parents agree to alternate major holidays.

When you choose a new place to live, consider your children. While the new home reflects your needs, it should also reflect their needs. For example, if they are used to open air, then a suburban environment will probably suit them best. The main aim should be to provide them with circumstances that will create a second home rather than a place to visit. You might want to include them in choosing your place to live.

This brings us to the second point. What do you do with them when they are with you? Many single parents fall into the trap of suddenly feeling they have to entertain and wait on their children, or buy gifts for them. Don't! When they are with you they should be required to be resourceful in entertaining themselves as well as pitching in and helping. This is somewhat contradictory, for you will probably have to plan in advance to create a "normal" setup for them. For instance, if there are no children their age nearby, encourage them to bring friends occasionally when they visit. For younger children, have a project they can help you with, such as choosing the menu for dinner and shopping for the provisions. Even asking them to do a little dusting or vacuuming is normal. You should be careful, however, to create a balance between work and play, and your children should have activities with their friends as well as alone with you. For older children, you should provide an activity that can induce communication—cooking dinner together, hiking, bike riding, picnicking, camping, etc.

One pitfall that many parents fall into is setting up a day or weekend of movies, amusement parks, zoos, and meals out. Some of this is fine, but a steady diet is unnatural. When deciding how to start off your new relationship, consider your children's everyday lives and try to duplicate this within your own new home.

Most away parents feel ineffective as parents. They no longer deal with the daily lives of their children and feel they have lost out in guiding their development and growth. Surprisingly, this need not be totally true. Instead of having to fool with the continuing small issues, the away parent will have an opportunity to set standards in major issues—mainly human relations. Let us be more specific. Children are noted for testing their parents. This does not diminish with divorce and often increases. They are inclined to test the away parent's love and durability.

Ann lived alone. Her children visited every weekend. After several months the children would demand to know what special activity she had planned for them each visit. "What goodie do you have for us today?" When they found that she insisted on some contribution from them in the form of "plans," they stopped coming for several weeks. It was hard, but she kept in touch with them, telling them she was available when they were, but on her terms. She was not going to be forced into bribing them. Eventually, they learned they could not manipulate her in this manner.

This vignette is not uncommon. Often children will test either parent by withholding themselves or their love. If they succeed, they are being taught manipulation and not honest, direct relating.

There seem to be three types of children that divorced parents have to deal with: (1) those who don't make much of an effort to keep up with the away parent; (2) those who try to monopolize the away parent; (3) those who strike a happy medium. There may be more than one type within a family. Have hope. Children who start out as one type may change with time if you keep in touch consistently.

If you wish to remain close to the child who does not make much of an effort, it is mainly up to you. All too often the away parent eventually drifts away from this type of child because of the lack of encouragement received. You are going to be required to have skin a mile thick and to be extremely flexible. You have probably been encouraging your children to live their lives to be independent, preparing them for adulthood. They pursue their own interests and contemporaries. You aren't a contemporary or even much of an interest. This hurts a great deal, but it's true. You will find that they probably will not call you often (or write, if you live away). You will usually have to make each overture. You may often be cut off from their activities that you normally would have attended. It is up to you to ask them continually what they are doing and jot these things down, telling them that you will be there. Ideally, the away parent should have communication from the at-home parent about upcoming activities of the children. It may be simply information or an actual invitation to an event—such as a football game, a dance, or a piano recital. The at-home parent is usually the only link between the very small child and the away parent. In divorces where there is only bitter communication, the away parent may have to make arrangements with the child's school, church, dance studio, etc., to be notified of events the child might be in.

Children's activities will come first before their visits with you. If you can be objective, think how many children stay home to be with parents on a Saturday night rather than go to a football game or spend the night with a friend. You might say here: "Wait a minute. I'm special because we see so little of each other." You aren't. This is a bitter pill that often makes parents give up. However, you need not. Flexibility, patience, and an occasional talk to your shattered ego can prevail.

Some parents have succeeded by first making their own plans so they don't leave whole weekends open for their children, only to be disappointed at the last minute. When planning, however, do leave some time open for the children, or even consult with them concerning the plans they have made. Several days before you hope to see them, or even on the day, work out an agreement. This requires weekly juggling, but it seems to be the best possible solution. Once the children are committed, hold them to it. If a better invitation comes their way, you might stipulate, "You said you were coming for dinner tonight; I'll expect you." This arrangement should also work two ways. Parents should not cancel out on their children at the last minute. In this manner, you will be teaching your children what a commitment means, but still giving them enough flexibility to pursue their own lives.

Don't forget that from time to time you should ask all the children how they like your visiting arrangements. Listen to any suggested changes they might offer.

The child who tries to monopolize the away parent will probably be working at you through your own guilt. These children are likely to be feeling your loss strongly and even blaming you and/or the other parent for their pain. They also might question your love for them. It is hard for parents who do feel responsible for their children's discomfort not to be monopolized. This type of child will call often, wanting to be with you and will often ask for material things. They may confide that they are not getting along well with the parent they live with. What do you do? You listen; you remain sympathetic; you assure them of your love through your concern. You see them often.

What do you not do? You do not drop everything and rush to them at each request. You do not buy them everything that they "have to have." You never undercut the other parent. If you become truly concerned about the family situation, you might want to speak to the other parent, but do so alone, remembering that you have heard only one side. Don't jump to conclusions. You must also let the children know that you have a life to live and that you are going to live it. They will be included, but they will not run it.

Marty called her father often to see what he was doing and to complain about Mother and how unpleasant she was these days. "Dad, I want to spend the weekend with you." Dad had made plans to go out on the river that Saturday afternoon. He found that he was in quite a conflict. He had made a commitment with his friends, but Marty needed him. He canceled his plans and had Marty over. She spent the whole weekend talking about how awful her mother was. He found that he couldn't help agreeing on some points, and told Marty so. The following week Marty called again. She needed a new dress for a dance coming up. Couldn't he take her out Thursday night to buy it? This time Dad had a business meeting that he canceled and Marty got her dress.

As you can see, this could go on forever unless Dad wises up. Marty had him both through the flattery of preferring his company to her mother's and through his guilt that when a person asks for help one must respond. However, Marty hasn't been learning anything constructive. Her father has been doing her a great disservice by adjusting his life exclusively to hers.

Children who strike a happy medium of keeping in touch with their away parent usually had a close relationship with both parents before the divorce. Often after the divorce both parents are able to remain objective and fair by encouraging the children to love and seek each parent. This kind of relationship usually must be nurtured by both parents. One simple statement of "Have a good time" from a mother sending her child for a regular visit with Daddy reassured the child that though her mother would miss her, she genuinely wanted her to have a good time with her daddy. No sad, long faces at the moment of departure.

One gesture to nurture a good relationship, where small children are involved, is for each parent to remind the child of the other parent's birthday, to mention that Mother's Day or Father's Day is coming up, or to send a card if one parent is in the hospital. As an ex-spouse, you may have no great desire to wish the other a happy birthday, but it won't hurt to encourage the child to do so. A homemade gift or card will be sufficient, or if the child has allowance money saved, help him spend it wisely on a gift. Truly here, it is the thought that counts. If this gesture is difficult for the parent, then grandparents or friends can help out.

The parent who lives with the children needs to give them frequent reminders to call or write the other or to seek the other out in various ways for help, advice, support, and companionship. These parents may even protect the other parent. It is easy for children to start depending on the parent they see every day, cutting out the other. It is up to both parents to help them strike a happy balance.

A child may have a question about homework. The at-home parent may say: "Call your dad. I'm not sure I know the answer to that." Or the parent may say: "It's been a while since you talked to Mom. Why don't you call and see if you can't work something out for the weekend?"

Obviously, this type of relationship is the best for all involved. Too often it is not achieved as children become the battlefield for parents' grievances toward each other. It is well to remember that everything said or done should be for the good and enjoyment of the child, not as retaliation upon the other parent. Keep your personal conflicts from clouding your judgment.

Martha had been divorced for three years. Her ex-husband lived nearby and had made consistent attempts to remain close to his child. Martha had not directly hindered by refusing to let him see the child, but she had occasionally made plans for entire weekends, deliberately cutting him off. She had never suggested to her child that he call his father for help on a school project or any of his activities. By these actions, she indirectly led her son to believe that Daddy really wasn't all that important or helpful.

Just as there are generally three types of children whom divorced parents have to deal with, there are three types of away parents the children have to deal with: (1) those who don't make much of an effort to keep up with the child; (2) those who try to monopolize the child; (3) those who strike a happy medium.

Some children will never have the experience of closeness with their away parent. The original home situation probably reflected the same scene. For many reasons an away parent may make little or no effort to see the children. Some may not have much love for any children, not even their own. Some may find it difficult to cope with a problem child or one who is handicapped. Some may be guilt-ridden over the divorce because of an affair and not be able to face the children. Though the child may be reaching out, there may be little response. There will be tears, disappointment, and frustration on the part of both the children and the at-home parent. Resentment is bound to mount. Successfully handling this is often difficult. For the small child, the at-home parent can try to encourage the away parent to show more attention. Older children can attempt to work more directly. All ages are sensitive and will have hurt feelings, but at least try not to set your child up for it. Don't buy a ticket for an event *expecting* the away parent to attend. Check first. Of course, this holds true for any existing relationship. Children will have to develop thick skin over the years, and learn to accept the fact.

On the opposite end of the spectrum, some away parents attempt to monopolize the child regarding visitation. If there is sufficient difficulty between parents who cannot agree and work out a satisfactory arrangement, having the court rule on specific visitation times may be necessary. Then the monopolizing away parent must operate within this framework. One away parent wanted the children every Thanksgiving and Christmas, in addition to the regular visitation. The "reasoning" was that the at-home parent had them during the week all year, and therefore he "deserved" to have them on these major holidays. Here is where a compromise is needed.

Children will react differently to being monopolized. They may feel guilty if they express to the away parent that they would prefer not to be with that parent so often. Enough of their own plans and activities going by the wayside may cause the relationship to be severely hurt. With other children, the home situation might be an unpleasant one; therefore monopolization by the away parent very well may be a relief.

Basically, with small children a problem of monopolization may need court intervention. Older children will usually be able to work things out directly with the away parent.

The away parent who strikes a happy medium of keeping in touch with the children usually had a close constructive relationship with them before the divorce. We have found it most encouraging to see a bond develop between a small child and the away parent as the years go on. Through healthy and consistent contact from the parent to the child, love is fostered between them.

DEALING WITH YOUR EX-SPOUSE

Many people take great offense at the word "ex." One divorced person avoided using the term by saying "the children's father." Even "former" wife or husband might make you more comfortable.

The definition of "divorce" in the *Webster's New World Dictionary* is "legal and formal dissolution of a marriage." While you have achieved or are achieving this through the legal process, the real separation from your partner is slow going and will take at least two years from the divorce. This may seem surprising and discouraging, but you will be undergoing a normal, healthy process that will leave you stronger and intact in the end.

In addition to a new relationship with your children, you will also have to work out an entirely new relationship with your ex. Perhaps you may wish that there were no need for a relationship at all, but this is possible only if there are no children or financial ties. On the other hand, you might find yourself hanging on to the past by trying to continue the relationship where you need not. Creating issues can be a way of hanging on. At the time, you may feel reasonable and justified. Your friends may agree. But usually where there is conflict, there is more than a casual relationship.

Agnes was very concerned that the children's father should not be allowed alone with them. He drank a great deal and had been arrested more than once for drunken driving. Consequently, she refused to let them see him. Many people would agree. On the surface, so would we. But what Agnes neglected to admit to herself or to friends was that while married he also drank but never around the children. Agnes was creating conflict by withholding the children, thus continuing the pattern of their old relationship of trying to "cure" him.

Susan had been the decision maker in her family by initiating the divorce. Joe reluctantly moved out. He amazed all their friends by adjusting rapidly. He became an open, cheerful person with many friends and interests.

Susan, on the other hand, struggled. Her adjustment and progress were slow. Eventually she became jealous of Joe. His newfound self often made her wonder if she had made a mistake. She took it out on him whenever she could. She withheld the children; she ran him down; and she created direct conflicts over money or any other issue she could find.

Susan, like Agnes, was still trying to continue the relationship as it had been. She had always been resentful of Joe and had spent her marriage trying to suppress his natural exuberance and enjoyment of life.

Even though you too may find what seem to be totally justifiable reasons to enter into conflict, you will have to learn to distinguish between continuing patterns of the old relationship and what really is justified. We will touch on this again shortly.

The divorce where there are no "hard feelings" is rare. During your marriage many bad feelings have developed. During the separation and the divorce proceedings they usually build to a crescendo of strong feelings. You have had to negotiate on matters that are extremely important to your future. You have had to try to reach an agreement with a person you probably find difficult to agree with on anything. From this antagonistic platform both partners after the divorce find themselves trying to work out arrangements concerning the children as well as other family matters. People who are divorcing or divorced seem initially to relate to each other with ambivalent feelings and actions.

You might hope or think that you are no longer interested in the other and don't need the person anymore. You will be surprised at your reaction when the other is still able to stir strong feelings within you. An example could be that although you are truly committed to divorce, you are amazed when your ex-spouse starts dating. You have irrational thoughts such as, How could he/she possibly enjoy or even wish to be with someone other than me? If your ex-spouse marries, you may experience an unexpected twinge. One woman was disturbed that the news of her ex-husband marrying made her feel funny and a little jealous. Through self-analysis she realized she was a bit envious of her ex-husband's starting out on a new life and apparently very happy. She did not want him back, but she did want a happier life for herself. When your former spouse does remarry, a major part of dealing with your ex is that of dealing with yourself. You are now in a whole new ball game. A new wife or husband also means a stepmother or stepfather for your children. You need to accept the fact that this person *will* play a distinct role. We encourage you to be fair and not to waste your time being difficult. Allow your children's stepparent to contact them and pick them up for visits with their away parent. Anything other than this will be unnatural and difficult for the children to understand. Try not to feel so threatened.

It can be an awful shock to find that your partner suddenly is changed from the person who still shared some goals with you to a person who seems completely working against you. This feeling could appear concerning the settlement proceedings as well as at other times.

You will also be amazed and become thoroughly disgusted with yourself when you suddenly find that you need to rely on the other for something such as advice or information. While in this phase, you will probably bounce from hurt to resentment, from anger to pure hate, to needing. This may last up to almost two years after the divorce.

It might be helpful to give you a glimpse of the goal you will be working toward. Ultimately you should be able to remember comfortably the happy moments you experienced together, as well as the unhappy times, without bitterness or anger. There should no longer be any need to strike out and hurt. There should be no curiosity about your ex-spouse's life. There should be no resentment. Actually, you should hope to be pretty much disinterested as well as remain unaffected by whatever the person does.

Even though you are able eventually to achieve this point of separateness, you did live with your ex for a number of years. You know him almost better than any other person and he, you. You went through many happy as well as trying times. A bond has been woven that will never really be severed. It has become a fine thread, but it is there. For example, if he has a crisis in his life, you may find that you respond even if just within your heart. It may not even take a crisis.

Mary and George had been divorced for four years. They had achieved the separateness of disinterest. The children were being picked up by their father on a visit to town. When he arrived they rushed out to greet him. Mary happened to look out of the window at this moment and felt a tremendous pang of empathy toward him. "How difficult not to be able to see the children daily."

One man stated rather succinctly: "Sure, there will always be a tie. I'd feel bad if a dog I had once owned was injured or killed."

Although separateness is eventually achieved, there will still be issues with which you will have to deal. Inflation will require renegotiating finances, or there might be a problem with one of the children. The parents may not agree and become annoyed and angry with each other. We have given examples earlier of conflict as a means for continuing the relationship; however, there can also be honest anger. If you find you are angry over an issue or incident, try to remove the personality of your ex-spouse. Would you be angry with another person who took the same stand, or are you allowing past grudges to cloud your emotions?

Earlier we touched on the point of how parents often use their children as weapons toward each other or as conductors of hurt. When two people live apart, the children are the easiest means to get at the other. How terribly sad. The away parent will be hurt if the children are encouraged not to see him or her, but eventually the children will be hurt much worse. You will be teaching them to be manipulative and unkind by withholding their affections.

Arriving at a workable relationship with your ex-spouse will take time, and the road may be rocky. Try to be fair and as objective as you can by having some regard for your ex-spouse as a person trying to establish a new life just as you are doing.

DEALING WITH FRIENDS, SOCIAL LIFE, AND RELATIVES

Friends are always valuable but particularly in times of crisis, and a crisis you've got! Close friends usually give a lot of support throughout the problems leading to divorce and may continue their support until your divorce is final. At this point, they sometimes seem to feel that their "duty" is over. Don't get your feelings hurt. Your situation is very similar to that of a patient who is in the hospital for many weeks. For the first two weeks the patient receives many cards, flowers, and visits from family and friends. All who are concerned about the patient want to let him or her know they care. Gradually cards and visits taper off, and the patient wonders if anyone really does care. Even family members who have come from out of town have had to return home. It is sometimes hard to realize that no one is really "down on you," but probably they all have their own life to lead or may be facing many personal problems.

Single friends are also a help. Some may have "been there" and can share experiences with you. They often are the ones you can call at the last minute when you need companionship. Ask them over for dinner or go to a movie.

We have found that a melding of single and married friends will give you better perspective and a well-rounded life. Just because you are divorced (or soon to be) doesn't mean you have to live an entirely single life. While you do have to make many changes, holding on to some things that were meaningful in your past is essential and healthy.

New friends will also begin to crop up as you get involved in new activities and your new life. These people will make you feel good. If you have been married for very long, you probably had mostly "couple" friends whom you and your partner saw together. The new friends will be all yours. This may sound a little elementary, but it is surprising what a good feeling it is to know that these people like just you.

We have discovered it to be a myth that a woman is usually the loser socially as the result of a divorce. Often it can be the other way around. Neither person need be the loser. There are a few friends who will take the initiative to continue to include you and keep in touch, but only a few. Even in this "enlightened" time, people still aren't sure what to do with or for divorced friends. It is up to you to show them. From your separation on, entertain. Married couples will respond beautifully to a single's overture. It will be difficult at first even to consider entertaining alone for both men and women, but do it. Your finances and previous experience will probably set the style from seated dinners to cocktail parties, or backyard cookouts, but all are fun. If you have a number of guests, let each couple do their own bartending. People will be glad to pitch in. Don't take on all roles, since you might not have help as you once did with your ex-partner when entertaining. By these means, you will be showing your friends that you are still interested in them and can handle situations alone. They in turn will feel comfortable about inviting you back without having to provide a date. Usually an invitation will give you the option of whether you want to bring a date or not. One woman found that her initial entertaining of married couples provided the opportunity for open discussion about her feelings on being invited to their homes. Her friends had wondered, and her ease in entertaining made them feel comfortable enough to inquire.

When entertaining or being entertained, don't allow yourself to belabor your own "state of affairs." No one wants to hear about your personal life and problems. It is boring, embarrassing, and dull, especially at a social function. On the positive side, keep abreast of current events so that you can participate in interesting conversation with your friends.

Your feelings toward your relatives may be somewhat ambivalent at times. You will often feel a need for their concern and support but also resent too much closeness. The old television commercial of "Please, Mother, I'd rather do it myself" comes to mind here. You will have to work out a happy medium of how much help you need and can handle. Family can play an important role in the lives of your children. If it is at all possible, strong family ties can help the children to feel less insecure and part of a group rather than "children who have to rely on only one person."

There are situations where relatives are many miles away or angry over your divorce and nonsupportive. If this is the case, it is best not to try to convince them of your position. Friends might become a substitute for you and your children.

CHAPTER 11

Dating

Can you believe it? Here you are faced with something you thought was long a thing of the past. You have been adjusting to the terminology (and the facts they represent) of "divorced person," "ex-spouse," and now it's "dating." A lot of people cringe at the word and what it represents. It's like high school again. Others look forward to dating. Some are afraid of possibly never dating.

We have noticed that dating seems to break down into certain stages:

1. Your initial reaction toward dating
2. Your revised attitude toward dating
3. Settling down to one person
4. Dating with the intent to marry

NOT ME

After separation some people find that they are not the least bit interested in dating. They have been too hurt and do not wish to chance that again. For some the divorce proceedings may take a long and drawn-out course, and some lawyers may advise against dating until all papers are signed and everything is final. When children are involved you may feel that they need some time to adjust to the idea of their parents' dating. On the other hand, some people need rest from the opposite sex. Association with groups of people or close friends is all they can handle at this time. It is easy to be rude to the opposite sex if you're needing your distance at this time. Try not to inflict your hostilities toward others because you feel "all men/women are alike."

Betty had not wanted to date. When asked out, she went but was nonresponsive and withdrawn. Not too many dates came her way. After almost a year of divorce she became aware that she had successfully met the challenges of her new life but still felt lonely. She had profound feelings that she was going to live forever—alone. She missed the feeling that she was important to another adult. It was time to take the risk. Immediately her attitude changed and the men she knew started calling.

COME OUT, COME OUT, WHEREVER YOU ARE

The right attitude and desire to date do not *necessarily* bring about such immediate results. One question most often asked by and of divorced persons is, "How do you meet people?" There are no pat answers. It often depends on the type of person you want to find and even what you're willing to go through. What works or is satisfying to one may not be for another. There are clubs to join, many that are specifically geared to a particular interest you might be pursuing, such as skiing, nature, boating. If your job affords little or no opportunity of meeting people, consider a change. More active participation in your church activities is another source of contact. A national organization called Parents Without Partners has been most rewarding for many divorced persons with children. For those living in condominiums or apartments, the pool and clubhouse provide many opportunities for meeting people. Let your friends know you'd appreciate their keeping you in mind for dates. Some people choose a "singles only" complex to ensure themselves of "datable" people. Singles bars are popular, but we found not ultimately rewarding. One must experiment according to one's own desires. You have to "dabble" in different areas, knowing that not everything will work out as expected or result in dating. Some efforts may even end in disaster.

Leslie had worked at her new job for several months and talked to many sales representatives, one of whom was especially courteous and attentive. He asked her out, and she readily accepted. Midway through the evening their conversation revealed her date to be a married man! She was mortified, since she had assumed him to be single, and there she sat in public in the very circumstance she most wanted to avoid. Where possible, don't be afraid to ask questions about a prospective date from someone who might know. Even ask the man himself, and hope you'll get an honest answer!

Beware of the married person who approaches you, for this is truly "barking up the wrong tree" and certain to cause trouble. Also, be careful of close married friends who "drop by" always offering to help. You may need help, but be careful whose you accept.

GO, GO, GO—A LITTLE DAB'LL DO YA!

Many people want companionship immediately after separation. Some feel the need for reassurance from the opposite sex that they are still appealing and attractive. Like Betty, they are not ready for the risk of strong emotional attachment. Often they find the means to provide the companionship without the risk of hurt or commitment. They may go to singles bars looking for dates. They choose people who are not compatible with their interests or backgrounds but who do provide an evening or weekend of fun. Some date people they had known before their marriage, trying to recapture something familiar, yet safe. Eventually all this will wear thin, just as Betty's singular position did. Having to adjust to different people continually gets to be tiring and unrewarding. Struggling to find a thread of common interest may make a person feel he is not himself.

I DON'T LIKE BEING SINGLE

Some people start dating immediately, looking for another mate. A word of caution. As previously stated, it will take at least two years to adjust to your divorce and new life. Planning to marry before the adjustment has taken place often ends in another tragedy. Much research has been done on this. The odds won't be with you. Use your common sense. Since your previous marriage failed, step back and take a good, long look at yourself and those you date. Don't rush into anything. There is plenty of time. Undoing is not nearly so easy as being cautious in the first place. Who wants another divorce?

WHY AM I DOING THIS?

After the initial fling or search, which may last a year or longer, you might find that dating is a drag—a hassle that you would rather avoid. It's now time to consider why you are dating. Your reasons may be changing. Do you want to date just to date, or do you want quality? You might find that you want the companionship of a person who means something to you other than a good time. You want somebody with whom to share your thoughts, feelings, and interests. You now know that you are attractive to the opposite sex and that you can get dates. You may discover that you cannot find a new partner just by looking, if this becomes your goal. If this is the case, your style will have to change. We have found that the meaningful relationships happen naturally. You cannot go out looking for them. If you are actively seeking a compatible person, you are not likely to find one. In our experience the rewarding close relationships develop when most unexpected. Often you will meet your "close friend" through other friends or even at work. You will have a base to build on—mutual friends, probably a mutual life-style, mutual interests and background. When faced with what we have just said, you may feel rather dismal. "I'm tired of the 'rat race,' but what am I to do in the meantime? Suppose I never meet anybody?" Many people continue to date but do so less frantically. They concentrate more on the other areas of their lives—the children, their homes, their jobs, interests, and friends.

At any point, during the process we have outlined, you may feel that you have met a person whom you really enjoy. You may date only him or her for months, or maybe even years. If eventually you find that things are not right for you, you may revert to your initial approach to dating and go through the whole thing again. This may happen many times.

No matter how many different dating relationships you have, you are in a constant process of discovering yourself. You may date people with different value systems, manners, dress styles, intelligence, goals, approaches of communication, etc. Because of these varying characteristics, you will be more serious with some than others. As you date an individual, you may determine immediately that this person is not for you and that even another date is out of the question. Or you may have enough interest to date for months, even years.

DOWN TO BRASS TACKS!

When people do find someone they want to date exclusively, with marriage as an eventual possibility, a great deal of enjoyment evolves as well as a lot of work. Most divorced persons are concerned about the possibility of "making the same mistake again." We are concerned with good reason. It happens often. During the period when you are becoming closer to a person you care for is the time to keep an eye on the methods of communication that you use and how successful they are. Here we all are again at the early warning signals stage. There will be times when your new relationship has its downs. There will be disagreements and problems to work out. Take your time. See if you are successful in working through things together. Many people are afraid to try new methods of communicating because of their past experiences. This is a time to learn. Talk about things and your feelings; be open, and attempt to relate to each other. You can't "predict" or assume each other's thoughts this early, as you could in your marriage. You need to discover each other. If you do not at least try to communicate, you run the risk of being turned on or off falsely. First impressions can work both ways.

By now you should know what went wrong in your marriage. Can you change your methods with a new partner? It is a thrill to find that you can. If you find the same patterns reappearing, give serious thought to the future. A professional might help you relearn. During this experiment in communication, don't get too analytical. Enjoy yourself. As in everything, there is a happy medium.

We are not saying that you are a "new" person. Nobody changes that much, but you can change habits and methods. Since you are essentially the same person, how will a new marriage work? Your new partner is not like your ex-spouse. He may enjoy qualities you have that annoyed the other. You may share interests and talents that were not in the first marriage. Also, you have a better understanding of what marriage means and will demand of you.

Be alert to the diversified responses you find in relationships with divorced persons who have no children, divorced persons with children, or persons who have never been married. One man, by going slowly, was able to see that marriage to his dating companion of two years would never work. She had never been married and had no children. He had two children, and in their particular situation could see that she could not cope with them even for the short periods of time the four of them spent together.

MOMMY, IT'S A MAN ON THE PHONE

Dating as a parent can be funny. It can also confuse the children. When you are dating different persons it is not always wise to include your children in this part of your life. No matter how old the children are, they will wonder if you are going to marry each person you go out with. Also, consider the adjustment you have to make with each new person. Why should your children have to make it too? You can meet dates for lunch or drinks after work "to check them out." If your children are accustomed to your going out with friends, they may not take too much interest in who picks you up as long as you don't wave a red flag by saying, "I have a date tonight." Beware of the person who tries to get to you through your children. On a first or second date, your friend might suggest a picnic or a trip to the zoo with your children. Get to know him better first. Some women try to involve men in their family lives as a means of hanging on to them. After one dinner with a two-year-old, you may never see that man again.

Once you have found a person whom you enjoy and wish to see often and who wishes to see you often, then you can gradually allow the intermingling. This is where it can get funny. Teen-agers are apt to be a bit embarrassed and therefore act uninterested in your relationship. They feel it is all right for them to date but find it awkward to see their parents dating. Smaller children are quite the opposite. Be prepared for questions or comments that may come up at the worst moments. Your child may turn to you in church and whisper audibly, "Mom, did Harry kiss you last night?" They may also test the honesty and durability of your relationship by announcing to your friend, "Mom slapped me last night," or "You should see Mom in the mornings—ugh!" Remember, they are establishing a new relationship, too. They may test your friend with disruptive behavior to see if he can last it out. Fun! One of the most embarrassing things, yet humorous, is when your child talks to your "date" about other men you've dated, even calling them by name. "Fred has a race car he takes Mom out in." "When John was sitting with Mom on the sofa last night. . . ." Or, "Your boyfriend is on the phone, Momma." All children may become jealous. "I don't like you. Go home." It's going to take patience and a lot of humor to get through this one. Even if it isn't that abrupt, it can be just as painful when the children aren't even civil to your date. Their rudeness and obvious displeasure can unnerve you. Be sure not to count on their helping you out at all.

Older children have the same questions and fears. They are not likely to voice them. When a new person moves into any family even on a dating basis, each child is going to have to find out where he or she stands. "Will I still be loved and needed?" One youngster, sensing that his mother was serious about George, asked quite definitely, "If you marry him, where will I live?" The mother inquired about his question, and he explained that he thought George would take her away, and he wanted to know with whom he'd be living. She reassured him that he would be included in any changes that would take place. He was very pleased to know this.

Go at it slowly. Don't rely on dates to entertain your children. Include them in some activities, and save others just for the two of you. This you should do forever after!

SHOULD I OR SHOULDN'T I?

Should you or shouldn't you what? You guessed it—sex! There is a lot assumed and said about divorcées and their sex lives. You may have read articles and books about nonmarital sex. Have you ever really thought what you would do if faced with options? Maybe fleetingly, maybe a lot, maybe never. Before you take a position or make a move, think and think hard. You will have to make decisions on two basic levels.

It seems to be somewhat of a laughing matter these days that a divorcée is willing, fair game either to married or single men and women. Some married people often find it their calling to console the poor frustrated divorcée. They want to offer "solace and comfort" in the form of their own bodies. Don't buy it! They are looking for either an easy way out of their own unhappy relationship or an anesthesia. You, in turn, will end up with heartache, a new spouse you married for the wrong reasons, or a bad reputation.

These people can be the spouses of your best friends as well as strangers. Their approaches can vary. A man may sidle up to a divorced woman at a cocktail party to whisper in her ear, "If you need anything, just call on me." A married woman might continually check in with a divorced man to "see how you are getting along."

The approaches may even be more overt. "I have admired you for years. I am very unhappy in my marriage and think we could really have a lot in common." If you do get approached by a married person, you are apt to feel terrible about yourself. "What did I do to bring that on?" Probably nothing. It's their problem, not yours. Keep it that way.

For most people who have divorced and are dating, the other question inevitably arises, "How involved should I get sexually?" The dilemma is understandable. You don't quite feel that an appropriate comparison can be made with your teen-age years and all the prohibitions that were laid out to you. You have become aware of your sexual needs during marriage. You may have anxiety about not having these needs met now that you are single. There should be very real and personal struggles that take place concerning your own moral beliefs, physical needs, and the demands that seem to be placed on "divorced persons" to be loose sexually or not be a part of the dating scene.

There are single people whose opinions about sex will be entirely different from yours. When you first date, you may not know what your opinions are and may be vulnerable to other ideas.

There will be frequent attempts to convince you that "there is nothing wrong with sex for sex's sake. Why not? You know what it's all about. All adults need sex."

Women can be made to feel frigid and question their own sexuality after a series of barrages of this sort. Men may feel compelled to prove their "manhood." Both may feel they will never be successful. Remember that sexuality can be undermined instead of enhanced if you are "bent" on proving it.

If you come to the conclusion that sex as a "meal ticket" or for companionship or escape is not for you, essentially what you are doing is choosing not to associate with people with values that oppose yours. There are others who will have values similar to yours. In this day those persons are usually harder to find, but they are still there.

How do you resolve the swirl of questions that may be darting back and forth in your head? One thing is quite certain. There are no easy and simple rules that will resolve the dilemma for you with no doubts remaining. There are some important things that you will need to bear in mind.

First, the whole issue of sex, as we have said, is more than simply intercourse. It is a matter of communication. If the communication is not deep, vital, and caring, then experience of sexuality will not be deep or vital either.

Second, since the meaningfulness of sex seems to revolve around that issue of "giving," then a very important issue to have in mind when considering sexual involvement is whether there is any duplicity or "using" of the other person in order to simply "get." Consider what the motivation is on the part of the other person. The motivation for sexual involvement is a good clue to the quality of the relationship.

In the "Go, Go, Go—A Little Dab'll Do Ya!" section, we dealt with the approach to sex as a need for sexual reassurance, or as a means for companionship without the threat of real intimacy. In these instances people are "using" each other.

Third, there seems to be more and more research demonstrating the likelihood that promiscuous versus committed relationships do have an effect on the richness of sexual experience. In other words, shallow relationships result in shallow sex. As you make plans for your future, injured by the failure of a marriage, we think it is important not to "set yourself up" for another failure by not taking the implications of sexual involvement seriously.

Fourth, the effects on other people of your becoming sexually involved are to be considered. In other words, are you willing to take responsibility for whatever effects your actions will have on others, such as children, friends, family? We are not talking about the old anathema of unplanned babies. It is far more than that.

You have a definite responsibility for setting the guidelines for your children's attitude toward nonmarital sex. If parents openly conduct a sexual relationship that their children are aware of, they must be prepared for their children to choose sex apart from marriage also. While you may be forty-two and feel that you are able to judge the quality of your relationship, they will not be able to see the difference between their age and yours and the level of maturity and experience. If you "do it," so can they.

Parents of your children's friends may no longer allow their children to come to your home if you have a person living there or sleeping there with you occasionally. Also, your children's other parent may have very strong feelings concerning this issue and be totally within their rights if they object.

What happens when you have a relationship where communication and mutual commitment have grown to the point where you feel deeply about the other person? If you have chosen not to become sexually involved during previous dating, you may find that you will want to reevaluate your stand. If it sounds as though we are making a big deal out of this, we are. It's your life, and your life is important. Making a big deal out of it means that you think matters through seriously because there are implications and ramifications for you. We aren't making the decision for you (as if we could!), but we are suggesting that you don't get into a heavy sexual involvement out of loneliness or the "mood of the moment." This is too important an issue for that.

DO I WANT PANTYHOSE IN THE BATHROOM OR WHISKERS IN THE BASIN?

At the time of divorce you may feel that you will never wish to remarry. You should certainly enter into divorce accepting that as a possibility. People who do divorce thinking "I'll find somebody better" are often off on the wrong foot from the start. They will be concentrating on looking for a new spouse rather than restructuring their lives.

We do not feel that remarriage has much of a chance unless other areas in your life have been developed first.

These are:

1. Understanding the problems in your first marriage
2. Understanding your contribution to these problems
3. Working out a satisfactory life-style for yourself
4. Working out a good relationship with your children
5. Developing a tolerable relationship with your ex (ex-spouses do have to be willing too)
6. Dating different types of people

If you feel you have successfully accomplished these steps, you will probably be living a rewarding life and not feel the need for remarriage. This is great, but what happens when you find yourself dating a person you love and with whom you think you might like to share your life?

In Chapter 1, "Early Warning Signals," we made some brief references to concrete indicators of "measuring" the health of a marriage. These same kinds of factors need to be used when you are deciding whether to marry again or not. There are many kinds of love that float around in this world of ours, and we are often tempted to get them confused. What are some of the kinds of love that *don't* make for a good marriage?

Obviously enough, the love that exists between parent and child is not the kind that makes a healthy marriage. There is a dependency there that makes for health in a good home environment but not for a quality marriage. There are also moments in which two people can move through a very harrowing experience together. Feeling joined together in facing some difficulty can be confused with marital love, but when there is nothing big to face, there doesn't seem to be much feeling left either, other than a residue of gratitude for having had each other in that big moment back when. Admiration and being admired can serve as another bad substitute for marrying love. Eventually one or the other will get tired of doing all the admiring and getting little in return.

Escape is not an uncommon reason for marriage. A person newly divorced is lonely. Why not find somebody to fill the gap? Finances can be tight. Each month is a struggle. Some people look for someone to help them out of this spot.

Hero worship can be confused with love. Look for the "true grit" in "the big man on campus," "the good-looking executive with lots of money," "the beautiful model type."

It's all right to feel sorry for someone, but it's not a good reason to marry. The more tangible issues are socioeconomic background, education, religion, and children. These examples may seem to be somewhat stereotyped, but nonetheless they appear regularly. Time is the best factor by which to evaluate any relationship. Unfortunately, time also makes it all the more difficult to break off a bond if it seems to fall into a classification like the above ones. But part of the process of finding out whether a relationship offers real promise is taking the risk of being wrong. Many divorced persons admit that they had moments before their marriage in which they were convinced that the bond was faulty; but after investing so much of themselves in it, they simply couldn't bring themselves to break it off.

When considering remarriage, you may have moments of sheer terror. You have adjusted to your new life and basically like it. You may loathe to give up your freedom. You may not want to take on the responsibilities of more children. You should give each anxiety serious thought. You may never *want* to remarry, or you may find that the sacrifices will be worth the gain. It is normal and desirable to have some doubts and concerns over remarriage as well as the relationship.

After adjustment from divorce and the creation of a new lifestyle some people become apprehensive over the demands that remarriage will require. If a lot of time has been given to the relationship, there will probably be some areas that concern one or both persons. There may be issues that cause discomfort and pain. If this is so, should the relationship be terminated? Not necessarily. In any marriage there will be pain and discomfort from time to time. If some of the circumstances appear before marriage, all the better. Both persons will have time to evaluate remarriage. Basically it's all a matter of degree. You should also face the fact that you may never remarry simply because the right person does not come along.

The real clues to the health factor, as you have probably learned to expect from us by now, fall in the area of mutuality and communication. Does the relationship seem to have a mutual give-and-take attitude? Is there a natural awareness of the other's needs and feelings most of the time? Does dependency shift between the two people in different circumstances? As the two people meet different situations, do the roles shift easily? Or do one or both seem locked into a permanent way of dealing with all issues? When decisions are made about places to go, things to do, ways to spend money, and priorities on time, is there compromise, or does one person seem always to control or always give in? Do you trust your personal welfare to the other? Are you willing to have your children model themselves after your prospective spouse? Have you worked out successful methods of communication?

One other warning. There is a tendency among many divorced persons to fall into a relationship with someone who either subtly or overtly has the same personality characteristics that you were unable to tolerate in your previous marriage. Explore new relationships carefully to see that that is not what is happening.